Coping With Bereavement

A handbook for teachers

John Holland

Cardiff Academic Press
St. Fagans Road
Fairwater
Cardiff CF5 3AE

© Cardiff Academic Press 1997

A catalogue record for this book is available from the
British Library.

ISBN 1 899025 05 7

Printed in Great Britain by
Antony Rowe Ltd, Chippenham, Wiltshire

Cardiff Academic Press Ltd.
with
Drake Educational Associates

To Joe and Rosie

Contents

Introduction

The aim of this book is to help teachers and other staff in schools to gain a greater insight into the difficult and often taboo subjects of death and bereavement. Through this greater insight it is hoped that staff will be better prepared to support bereaved children, and also to help prepare all children for the bereavements which they will encounter at some point in their lives.

The book was written as a result both of direct teaching experience, mostly in the primary sector, and also of research in both primary and secondary education. The author has also been involved in training programmes supporting teachers and schools.

Research showed that death and bereavement were uncomfortable topics for many teachers and were identified as areas where more training was required. Bereavement expertise in schools was generally sparse, with most teachers having little pre- or post-qualification training. As the Code of Practice (DofE, 1994) acknowledges that children may be affected by emotional and behavioural difficulties, as encountered by bereaved children, this is an area which needs to be addressed, as these children are potentially part of Warnock's 20%. (DES, 1978)

The book is divided into three parts. In part one, death and bereavement are considered in the context of losses generally and of attachment bonds, in particular.

The second part of the book discusses a pro-active approach to help develop strategies to deal with and address the issue of death, loss and bereavement in the school curriculum.

The third part of the book considers a re-active approach, to help deal with problems arising after a child has been bereaved. It includes ideas as to how immediate help can be offered to the child and also offers information on where to find advice and speedy secondary help. Finally, the book addresses the need to develop whole school policies and contingency plans which should ideally be in place to deal with a sudden and unexpected bereavement.

The book is not intended as a replacement for the skills of the bereavement counsellor, but rather as an awareness-raising book which gives some direction and structure to the topic. Although much of the material in this book is targeted at the primary education sector, an age when many children will still be developing a concept of death, it is also relevant, with adaptation, to the secondary sector too. Each chapter ends with useful follow-up activities for staff which can be used to form part of a training programme.

Part One: Death, Loss and Culture

Most children, thankfully, do not go through the trauma of the death of a parent. Although being in a minority, these children still form a sizeable group. Wells (1988) estimated that forty children a day in England and Wales are bereft of a parent, and that there are around two hundred thousand such children in Britain. Holland (1993) in a study of Humberside primary schools, found that over seventy per cent had at least one child bereaved of a parent or significant close relation within the previous two years. A follow up study in Humberside secondary schools by Holland and Ludford (1995) found a similar high rate of bereavement. For children, touched by the death of a parent or a sibling, bereavement is a highly relevant issue within their actual experience. They may be lonely and isolated, their peers and adults, at home or at school, may not provide the understanding or support needed. Quiet children may be perceived as 'coping', in contrast to potential inner turmoil and depression. Others may display bad behaviour resulting directly or indirectly from the bereavement.

Most children will face the death and bereavement of relations or friends in their life, and preparation for bereavement, in the context of this being a life skill, similar to sex education, can take place in a non morbid way. If teachers and schools address the topic in a positive manner, children should be better able to cope when confronted with death. It will also allow children to develop an empathy and understanding of their bereaved peers.

CHAPTER 1

Death and Loss

Bowlby (1973) was one of the first to highlight the area of loss and its consequences. Much of this early research was carried out with animals, but it identified some significant issues which were important in later studies of humans. These included the importance of the bonding process and the potential consequences of offspring failing to achieve a successful bond.

The notion of loss revolves around the concept of an individual establishing a relationship, or an attachment bond, with either somebody or with something. This attachment bond may be established slowly over a period of time, or can occur quite quickly, as with new born babies bonding with their mothers. The mother, of course, has the months of pregnancy when she is carrying the child to begin her bonding process. Another example of an attachment bond is when we first meet a potential partner and gradually become more emotionally attached to them.

When loss occurs, it is this attachment bond which is broken, sometimes unwillingly or suddenly without warning. It is the breaking of this bond and the ensuing problems which come under the term 'loss. In many cases of loss, matters are quickly resolved and the individual eventually recovers. The breaking of the attachment bond will cause a mourning reaction and a grief process begins, ending only with the eventual resolution, when the loss becomes fully integrated into the life of the individual affected. The length of time this process takes, and the level of trauma suffered by the individual, will depend on a variety of factors, including the depth of the attachment bond, the manner in which it was broken and how long the relationship lasted.

How an individual copes with loss also depends on a variety of factors, including the control they have, their previous life experiences, the support systems they have around them, their coping strategies and their preparations for dealing with loss.

Bond formation and breaking

It is perhaps no surprise that many of our cultural euphemisms for death revolve around words such as 'loss or 'lost. Such euphemisms attempt to lessen the impact of using the word 'death', with its implications of finality. Euphemisms bring with them their own problems and while they may be clear to adults, they can easily confuse children. Death is the ultimate breaking of an attachment bond and potentially more traumatic than any other form of loss. Death is significant in that it is irreversible. It will also be especially momentous if it involves a significant other, such as a partner, parent, sibling, child or very close friend. In principle death is no different from any other loss experienced in life, though it is likely to be of much greater intensity.

Death is far from the only loss which individuals will encounter during their lives. It has been suggested that developing the ability to cope with these other losses helps us to better cope with deaths and bereavements which we will encounter later in life.

The rest of this chapter discusses a variety of losses we may experience in different areas of life and how these experiences can affect our coping strategies.

Family relationship losses

The changing or breaking up of family relationships involves the issue of loss. These relationship losses are potentially traumatic, and may include family feuds, separation and divorce. Other things can disturb the balance of family relationships such as the arrival of a new baby. This may seem to be only a positive and happy event for all involved, but it too can bring a measure of loss. If the baby is the first child, then the established relationship between the parents can be thrown out of equilibrium, as the new parents have to make adjustments to cater for the demands of the new arrival. If the baby is not the first, then it is not only the relationship between the parents which will be thrown out of equilibrium, but also the relationship between the parents and existing children. Everyone in the family unit has to adjust to the new status quo. In both situations it is highly likely that each family member will suffer some degree of loss. The parents only have so much attention to divide between the total family and each other, and as a result the established family members may find that they receive less attention. The family focus, at least initially, will be on the new arrival. Both the children and the adults may find these changes difficult. These changes are permanent and things can never be the same again, but usually the family will adapt to the new equilibrium. With further changes later in their lives, the equilibrium may again be thrown out of balance, so the family system is a dynamic one.

Children rarely experience these changes in the same way as adults. Adults have an additional issue of control in their favour, while for children any changes may seem unpredictable and unforeseen. Children cannot predict the impact of the arrival of a new brother or sister, or anticipate the period of adjustment.

For them, the period from the change in circumstances to the restoration of the family equilibrium can be described as a period of mourning. In a well functioning family this period will soon pass and a new equilibrium will be found in which all family relationships are restored.

While the addition of a new member to the family unit affects the equilibrium, as discussed, there are other changes to a family unit which can have more serious, long term affects.

The rate of divorce or separation of couples has greatly increased over the past few years. One implication of this increase is that a large number of children may well lose permanent contact with one of their parents, at least throughout their childhood.

This represents a significant loss for both the child and the absent parent. The loss is complex. It is not final, as with a death, so it remains unresolved and can have the potential for long term problems.

The age at which the separation occurs is also significant. The affect on a young baby may be minimal, in terms of the loss of a carer, and the effects may be very short term. In comparison, a similar loss for a school-aged child, where the loss may involve an individual with whom a solid bond has been established and who is seen as a role model, has the potential to cause, long term damage. Often, it is not until they become an adult that this childhood loss is finally addressed. They may try to find the parent, which can also be the case when adoption has taken place, in search for some sort of meaning to what they experienced.

Although divorce and adoption do not have the finality of death, they may present both short and longer term problems for children. Similarly, bereavement through death will have long term implications, if grieving is not successfully resolved.

There are other changes in the family that are not generally recognised as being traumatic but which can still dramatically affect the equilibrium. When a child first leaves the family home, such as to attend nursery or begin school, this involves a loss for both child and parents. The child may be reluctant to leave the security of the home and the parents too may miss the presence of the child during school hours. In later years there will be similar losses, for example, when the child changes classes and has a new teacher, when they move from primary to secondary school and so on. Later, during adolescence, there will be another period of loss. For the young adult this includes the loss of childhood and the loss of the security of their parents, as they are now expected to stand on their own two feet and become more independent. These elements of loss are in addition to losing childhood innocence, as puberty and sexuality arrive.

Finally, when the young adult leaves the family home, either to go to university or set up on their own, further losses are felt. For the parents there will be an empty room, changes in the family routines and a substantial reduction to the nurturing role. In addition, the parents may now have to address relationship problems between themselves that were 'shelved' during the child-rearing stage of their relationship. The young adult will now begin to grow towards further independence and, in the likely event of finding themselves a partner, will further change the child-parent relationship.

There are many other types of losses which we may experience, affecting our family relationships. These may include a loss of sexual functioning, the inability to mother or father a child, illness and miscarriage. The inability to produce a much desired child, or grandchild, is as much a loss as a stillbirth, miscarriage, abortion or birth of a disabled child. In all these cases there is the loss of a potential, or of a perceived 'ideal' future, the loss of 'what might have been'.

Relationship losses, not within the family

There are similar types of relationship losses which follow this general pattern but are not within the context of the family. These relationship losses include 'breaking up' with a boyfriend or girlfriend, losing touch with a once close friend and 'leaving behind' old friends and/or colleagues when moving to a new area or job.

We can become very attached emotionally to a group of individuals, such as school friends, peers at college and colleagues at work. In these settings there will have been many shared and joint experiences and when we have shared both adversity and elation with other people, over a period of time, we can suffer a loss or grief reaction when the group breaks up. This may be at the completion of a course, when we change jobs or if we move to a new area.

Other personal life losses

Losses can also occur when we become unemployed, are made redundant or eventually retire from work. In such cases, adjustments will have to be made to our life and there may also be economic and psychological damage. There may be other losses, such as a decline in our social or economic status, as we are no longer in the role of 'worker'.

We can also suffer loss of freedom or loss of choice in our life, through imprisonment, being admitted to hospital, having a serious illness, etc. These will cause a change of routine in our life and, as a result, we may well find that some of life's options are no longer available.

Physical loss

Abuse of any sort, physical or emotional, embodies the loss of both innocence and self-esteem. A grief reaction can be induced by partial loss to an individual, for example, through physical damage causing a disability, injury or illness. At the extreme of disability there may be a physical loss through the amputation of a limb or through a condition that prevents us from being involved in activities which we had previously enjoyed. A heart condition or a stroke, for example, may force us to limit a previously energetic sporting pastime. We may even suffer losses of physical functioning such as speech, memory, intellect or mobility, or suffer a disfigurement after an accident or operation in hospital.

'Self' loss

For whatever reason, we may also lose our religious faith, or we may lose our personal hope and future expectations. At many times in our life we may suffer a loss of confidence, usually following a particularly bad experience. This may make us question ourselves and our beliefs. Our self-esteem will be 'knocked' and we may seriously begin to doubt ourselves and our abilities.

In all of the examples presented here, there has been some form of attachment, or anticipation of attachment, which has been breached. This will be followed by some sort of regret, grief or mourning reaction. Usually, there is a final resolution of the loss, as the loss becomes integrated into our life. Unfortunately, even over time, the loss is not always resolved and individuals may need special help, such as counselling, to work through any unresolved issues.

Loss, animals and artefacts

We can develop very close attachments to things other than people in our lives, such as our pets. A child or adult may have a very strong bond with their pet cat, dog or hamster. The subsequent loss of this pet, if it has literally been lost or if it has died, may well generate a grief reaction in the owner and the extended family.

Loss can also be expanded to include inanimate objects, both large and small, such as a house, country, car, souvenir, certificate, book or favourite photograph. We can suffer a loss even when we move house, not just the obvious loss of our home but also that of our neighbours, social network and daily routines. If we move a great distance, such as emigrating to another country, then we may suffer further compounded loss in terms of culture and our 'roots', as well as of our family and friends whom we may no longer be able to visit easily.

One factor in the extent and intensity of the grief which is suffered, will be the degree of our attachment to the objects. The common feature in loss is this attachment bond, its being broken and then the subsequent grief reaction.

Compounded losses

Losses do not always occur individually, as isolated cases, but they can often be connected. If more than one loss occurs at the same time then this is a multiple or compounded loss. We may, for example, move house at the same time as losing the family cat and having the furniture removers break a much treasured artefact. We may have a traumatic relationship breakdown and experience divorce, lose contact with our children and suffer the loss of our home and neighbours.

The depth of the loss reaction will depend on many factors, including the strength of the attachment bond and the manner in which the bond is broken. How we deal with the little losses in life will be one component which will determine how we cope with bigger losses, such as a bereavement. For example, if we cope successfully with a temporary separation from our parents when children, like staying at a friend's house for the weekend, this will help us to cope with future losses in life. Ward (1989) contended that our ability to cope with any crisis will, generally, depend on how well we are prepared. Parents may attempt to shield their children from life's little losses, such as rushing out to the pet shop to replace a dead goldfish, without sharing the news of the pet's death. The parents are missing a useful, experiential opportunity of helping the child to successfully cope with a little loss, with the potential to help them prepare for later, larger losses.

Follow-up Activities

1. Can you remember when you first started school, primary or secondary?
   What were your feelings?
2. Brainstorm as many of life's potential losses as you can, within three minutes.
3. How did you feel when you first left home to go to college or move into your own home?
4. Recall some of the happy memories you have of your first home.

CHAPTER 2
Death and Culture

Death - the taboo

Death is the one certainty of life, we all die eventually. There is no escape for anybody from their eventual fate of dying; no one is immortal. With the inevitability of death, it is perhaps a puzzle as to why death also seems to be one of our greatest cultural taboos. Death is not a topic generally discussed, but rather one which tends to be actively avoided. Golding (1991) contended that death is regarded as a topic to be avoided in polite conversation and around which negative attitudes tend to prevail. Perhaps, subconsciously, we think that if we ignore death then it will reciprocate, building up a psychological defence mechanism.

It is generally accepted that we avoid talking or thinking about unpleasant issues. We may avoid thinking about where meat comes from, as we prepare it and eat it, avoiding thoughts of the animal being slaughtered. We may avoid thinking about why people in the world suffer gross depravation, despite our high technology, relative affluence and over production of food.

These are subjects which we prefer to ignore, along with death, pretending that they don't exist and without giving them much thought. Not addressing such issues usually stems from anxiety and fear of the unknown. As a result, death, by and large, is ignored until it strikes at our immediate, personal circle.

Death in our past

Our so-called 'civilized' society is one in which death has developed into more of a taboo subject than it was in the past. In the last century, people were much more used to dealing with both death and bereavement. Past generations have had to endure the great epidemics, such as cholera outbreaks, typhoid and the 'Black Death', which often raged, bringing death to large proportions of the population. Death was far more a visible part of their everyday lives.

Life expectancy at birth was then relatively short due to poor medical conditions, lack of emergency care provisions, food shortages and the epidemics.

The death of the 'bread winner' would, in these earlier times, have had dire consequences on the family leaving them destitute and dependent on the support of others. There were none of the 'safety nets' now in place in terms of insurance provision and state support.

Things are very different today, at least in our western culture, as infant mortality has declined and life expectancy at birth has risen.

A cultural change?

Marris (1974) described how death and mourning, in Victorian times, were covered by a precise social convention and formula. During these times there was no doubt or confusion surrounding what one should do when someone died. Everyone knew exactly what was expected and also what would follow after a death. 'Full mourning' included the complete shuttering of the family house and the wearing of black clothes by close family, for a prescribed period. The time and depth of mourning would depend on how close the actual relationship was between that of the mourner and that of the deceased. The Victorian age was perhaps, at least in our own culture, the culmination of bereaved-led mourning, epitomised by the mourning of Queen Victoria for Prince Albert, from whose death she never seemed to recover. The modern death movement in the United States is, in some ways, similar to our experience in the Victorian age.

This approach contrasts with much earlier ages, and also with some cultures and religions today, where the emphasis is only indirectly on the mourners and focussed far more on the deceased. The focus was on the right of passage of the deceased as they made their journey to an existence after life, following death. The past cultures of Egypt, China and the Vikings all provide examples of the focus being on helping the deceased through this transition. The Egyptians built massive structures, the pyramids, for their dead Pharaohs and left valuables and equipment, as well as slaves, for them to use on their journey to the after-life.

While the focus was on the deceased, the bereaved seemed to gain comfort from these rights of passage, knowing that 'the traveller' was on a journey to a desired destination, which they would make safely because of the provisions made.

There are other differences when we compare our attitudes towards death with those in the past. In the past, the body of the deceased would normally be 'laid out' in the home of the family. The body would be retained in the house until the time of the funeral and subsequent burial, and friends and relatives would come and 'pay their respects' to the deceased. Children would naturally be involved, in an incidental way, with the death and mourning process. This would especially be the case when the death concerned a close family member or a sibling. They would also hear all about death in incidental conversations of adults, as death was not hidden from them, and was just a natural part of an everyday topic.

Death as a contemporary experience

The frequent opportunities to observe death close at hand, as in the past, now no longer exist. Today, neither children or adults are likely to have encountered death either as frequently or at such close quarters as they would have done in the past. In contrast, today, there seem to be few rules, norms or conventions to provide guidance in what to do following a death. This lack of knowing what is expected can lead to uncertainty regarding how to act and how to respond. Such uncertainty may mean that the bereaved are so unsure as to how to proceed, that they simply choose not to respond at all. This can lead to an over-reliance on the professionals available.

The area of death, as with many other areas in life, now seems to have been 'professionalised', sanitised and removed from the context of the family. Professionals have made considerable inroads into the functions that were once previously provided for within the extended family unit. In this way they seem to have claimed a special knowledge, creating further mystery and fear around the topic of death. Undertakers are a relatively recent profession, to 'undertake' the unpleasant side of death on our behalf.

After a death, the professionals are likely to quickly be at hand, offering advice and taking control. They will remove the body of the deceased from the home, although, in contrast with past generations, the body is more likely to be in a hospital or hospice. Walter (1990) recalls that it is only since 1945 that most deaths have taken place outside the home.

Once the body of the deceased is removed it is taken to a morgue or funeral director and chapel of rest. Nowadays it is rare for the body to be returned to the family home, except perhaps just before the funeral,

14

in the cortege to the church, crematorium or similar.

This change in procedure means that the family, including the children, no longer have easy access to the body of the deceased. As a result by the time the funeral takes place it may seem very impersonal, cold and clinical.

While the funeral still holds its place as a public recognition of the death, with some religious aspect, nowadays it is less likely to take place close to the home. It may be in a busy, central church or crematorium. The service is likely to be short and part of the daily timetabled services, just one of a queue of funerals to be held.

It may be that funerals only survive today, not so much as a ritual for the deceased or the bereaved, but merely as a function for disposing of the body. Matters seem to be rushed along and sorted out as quickly as possible, with as little fuss or embarrassment as possible. The benefits of this 'streamlined' procedure to the bereaved is perhaps questionable.

Family structure

Another factor that affects how people cope with death today may well relate to the contemporary family structure. Families nowadays do tend to be far more dispersed geographically than was previously the case. Families may be in relatively isolated single units, especially as many families today are nuclear, perhaps even with only one adult member. This contrasts with the past where families were often closer geographically and more support was therefore available from the 'extended family' circle.

Family systems today often provide far less direct support to those bereaved than they would have done in the past, when there were stronger and more supportive family links close to home. Families in the past tended to remain within a limited locality, with the obvious exceptions of some of the great migrations and mass emigrations. Grandparents, uncles, aunts, cousins and other relatives often lived close at hand and would all have been available to give vital support to the bereaved when needed, at these and other times of crisis. There seems to be far more potential for the bereaved to be isolated in our modern times, than in the past when society, as a whole, was far more static and stable.

Friends and family may still, as in the past, provide a support network, though it is more likely to be by odd telephone calls, occasional visits and letters. This modern day support isn't always available as and when the bereaved needs it, in comparison to the times when everyone in the village knew each other and rallied around to help, giving direct support.

Improvements in science

Science has extended the boundaries of life and increased our average life expectancy. In our culture, science has eradicated famine and provided consistency and reliability in our food supply, as well as providing us with a potentially improved diet. We are now unlikely to die from a simple illnesses, such as malnutrition or diarrhoea, which kill thousands of children in developing countries of the world.

Nowadays it is less likely that we will have had the sad experience of losing either a sibling or parent during our childhood. We may even only experience the death of a grandparent or parent relatively late on in our life.

Medical science can now prolong life far longer and we have a far greater chance of surviving an accident, serious illness or medical condition.

It may be that our thresholds of expectations, and therefore also our accepted 'norms', have been altered. Today, when a death does occur, it may be against all our expectations. We assume that the medical profession will eventually prevail over the illness, injury or condition. When a death does occur it may now be perceived more as a failure; a failure of medical science and technology; to sustain the life of the deceased and keep the 'grim reaper's scythe' at bay.

Secular society

Another factor which may well contribute to the depth of loss felt by the bereaved, is that our society is far more secular than in the past. We tend to be less religious, at least outwardly, with far less people regularly attending church or other religious places. This decline in faith can perhaps be traced back to the growth of science, in particular the theory of evolution disputing the belief that God created the world and mankind. As a result, the growing number of non-religious people whose belief system does not acknowledge the existence of an after-life, have no answer to the fundamental question, 'What now?'

Death may be perceived as a final event, the end, rather than the start of an after-life in 'heaven'. This can make the loss appear even greater as there is no comfort gained by the thought that there is something 'beyond' and that the deceased has merely gone ahead to a 'better place'.

The post funeral professionals

There may be quite a lot of support for the bereaved around the time of the death and the funeral. However, this support may wane substantially over time, as both the friends and relations believe the grieving period is coming to an end. They may grossly underestimate the length of time the bereft person needs their support.

People may become unwilling or unable to give their patient support in the medium and long term and the bereft person may discover that people find contact with them an embarrassment. The support network may withdraw fearing that they will somehow upset the bereaved, not knowing what they can say or do to help the situation. Any conversations which take place later on may be on a very superficial level, as people may even avoid mentioning the deceased person's name or any subject which may be linked to them.

In sharp contrast, the last thing which the bereft individual may want is to be left in isolation, without their loss being acknowledged. They may even find people crossing the street to avoid contact, such is their uncertainty of how to interact. Lewis (1961) gives an account of incidents encountered by the bereft, which are contained in his book, 'A Grief Observed'.

He writes that the bereft individual may have a desperate need to articulate their loss and that this need may be denied by their immediate circle of friends, at least after the initial period of the death and funeral. Talking about the deceased and the death not only acknowledges the loss but also helps the bereaved to work through their grief. Watson (1986) also related the importance of this following a tragic accident in which he was the sole survivor of a family of five.

Bereavement and grief seem today to be seen as an illness rather than as a natural reaction to loss. Grief has to run its course and will usually, in time, be resolved.

Where immediate support is not forthcoming from friends or relatives, the bereaved can turn to voluntary or institutionalised counsellors and supporters. They are able to respond to situations of crisis, and really only exist to fill the void which has been left by a society that has all but lost the social and cultural skills of dealing with the areas of grief, death and mourning.

The voluntary organisations include Cruse, The Compassionate Friends and The Samaritans. Alternatively, through self-referral, or referral through a GP, the bereaved may receive professional help from a counsellor, psychiatrist or psychologist.

Second hand death in the media

Another difference in our experiences of death and bereavement today, compared with people in the past, is the amount of media coverage death now gets.

While perhaps avoiding the issue in our personal lives, we encounter death on a daily basis through the media, via television, radio, newspapers, books and the cinema. This media-type of death is ubiquitous and is often represented in both fact and fictional death. No self-respecting action film today lacks frequent examples of death, often spectacular, grisly and violent. Unfortunately this provides an unbalanced perception, that death and violence are intrinsically connected, which is simply not the case. Kubler-Ross (1982) points out that, today we subconsciously perceive death as 'being killed' rather than simply dying of old age or natural causes.

If we are so exposed to death in the media, why doesn't it help to ameliorate the apparent taboo surrounding death? At the margin it may well assist, reminding us of our eventual fate, but also it can become so familiar to us that we simply don't internalise it and it remains ignored other than at the subliminal level. Some films, such as 'Ghost', 'Always' and 'Truly, Madly, Deeply', actually go beyond the death issue and address bereavement and mourning. However, even here they provide an unrealistic, comforting reassurance and sentimental hope of a 'wished for' scenario of life after death.

Perhaps we do not make connections between media death and our own destiny. Death is always something which happens to somebody else.

In relation to media fiction, we know only too well that the actors taking part are only acting and that in reality they don't die. Children watching such fictional deaths may be reassured that the death isn't real. This can lead to confusion in the long term as children begin to perceive death as not actually being real or final.

With regard to factual death reported in the media, we are often shielded from the true horrors through the system of censorship. For the vast majority of viewers and listeners, these brief encounters with death are not 'first hand'. They are observing scenes from a safe distance and are often separated by both time and space from the reality of the death. They are experiencing death at a 'second hand' level.

Ultimately, if the media portrayal becomes a little too close for comfort, we can simply switch off the radio or television and distract ourselves with something else. We can avoid experiencing any sense of loss. We have established no attachment bond with the deceased, we do not have to attend the funeral and we can avoid experiencing any sense of loss or grieving.

We may even avoid thinking about those individuals for whom the death is directly relevant. The media intrusion into their lives can potentially impose an additional and unwanted strain on them at a time of great shock, stress and vulnerability.

Death in other cultures

Our treatment of death contrasts sharply, not only with our own past, but with other cultures in existence today. In some other cultures the body of the deceased is retained within the family setting for a period of mourning, and at times this mourning can be frenetic. Often the mourning involves all the immediate family, relations and friends, and includes both adults and children. Greater community and religious significance may be attached to the death and bereavement, in which the bereft finds additional support and comfort to help them through their period of mourning. In some communities the emphasis is still very much on the right of passage for the deceased instead of those 'left behind'.

The English culture does tend to be one of reserve at such times of stress and in contrast to many cultures, avoids making any 'fuss'. We have the 'stiff upper lip' syndrome, remaining calm and composed at times of great stress and not revealing our true feelings. Males in particular, and probably to their emotional cost, are expected to be stoical amongst the utmost tragedy, offering support and strength. Females in our culture are at least allowed some degree of freedom when it comes to showing their feelings, but even here there are limits drawn regarding intensity and time. It is far from the open wailing and grieving acceptable, even expected, in some other cultures.

Being unaccustomed to such open grieving we may find it difficult to understand and even embarrassing, but it can actually be very positive and therapeutic. Our general attitudes contrast greatly with the approach even in some places relatively close at hand, such as in parts of Ireland, where a wake may be held providing both community and family support for the bereaved. This tradition is also found in places where there is a strong Irish influence, such as London and Liverpool.

Other groups are also far less reserved and will outwardly show their grief. For example, in West Indian cultures the body of the deceased is likely to be kept in the family home before the funeral and the bereaved family friends for months following the funeral. The bereaved family are provided with support and comfort over a longer period of time.

The major religions of today have many differences in their responses to death. There seems to be a general division between the religions of the West, such as Judaism, Christianity and Islam, and those of the East, including Hindu, Buddhist and Sikh. The Western religions tend to place a far greater emphasis on the body in their ceremonies while Eastern religions emphasise the spiritual side of the bereavement. It is difficult to make generalisations about any religion, as there are many sects adopting varying practices within each religion. In the case of uncertainty regarding religious implications, the family should always be consulted to determine what is, or is not, appropriate in the circumstances. Specialist books on the various religions should be consulted for a more detailed approach.

Judaism

In the Jewish religion, the oldest of the eminent monotheist religions, there is a duty to be present with the dying, as there is a duty to honour one's parents. After the death, Orthodox Jews will not be cremated, but buried in a complete state. The burial will take place very quickly, usually within a day of the death, in consecrated ground. Some Jews return to the Holy Land, in particular the city of Jerusalem, to be buried. Initially there was some belief in a resurrection, which resulted in the desire to be buried intact. This view of resurrection has been modified in some sections, to the survival of the soul after death. It is only following the burial that the period of mourning can commence.

The Jewish religion has the week of mourning, 'Sitting Shiveh', which is an intense period of mourning. Those bereaved traditionally sit on low chairs, remaining indoors with garments rent. All daily routines are suspended, mirrors covered and curtains drawn. The mourners are united in their grief and emotional outburst is expected in this initial period of mourning. The children are highly likely to be included in the mourning proceedings, as a matter of course.

The dead are often remembered in the names of new members of the family born after the death.

There is a strong community support at the time of the death and on the anniversary, 'Yahrzeit', which becomes an important focus for the period of mourning.

Islam

Islam is one of the most widespread of the world's religions and has drawn much from Judaism. The Muslim has five duties in life, which include daily prayer, observing Ramadan and making a pilgrimage to Mecca at least once during their lifetime. Muslims believe in a physical resurrection at the Day of Judgement and therefore are buried intact, rather than cremated. The burial takes place as soon as possible after death, as with the Jewish religion. The period of mourning can last for up to three months and the children are involved with the funeral and following mourning rituals.

Hinduism

The Hindu religion, the most common in India, has a strong central belief in reincarnation. The belief is that the soul transmigrates to another body where it starts a new life. Life is seen essentially as a cycle of lives and an individual's destiny is determined by their deeds, with the ultimate goal being that of absorption. The Hindu religion also has a very strict system of castes.
The purpose of the funeral in the Hindu religion is to set the soul free, to enable it to be reincarnated in another body. Another central belief is that the length of life is predetermined and, in a sense, any deaths which occur are at an appropriate time as that life has run its preordained course. These factors, along with the likelihood of there being a strong community support, will comfort the family and friends of the deceased. The tradition is for the body to be cremated and children are generally included in the rituals as a matter of course.

Buddhism

Buddhists, as with Hindus, tend to have a very strong affinity with the cycles and changes of life. Birth and death are accepted as being parts of these cycles and there is the belief that eventual absorption of the soul will be accomplished through the mediums of ethics and discipline. Acceptance of the inevitable is again a comfort for the bereaved and, as with the Hindu religion, cremation is part of the culture. Children are allowed to join in with the rituals and processes following death.
In Tibet, Buddhism developed into Lamaism with the belief of reincarnation of the Dalai Lama. After the death of the body of the Dalai Lama, the spirit is believed to transmigrate to a new body, and a search

is then commenced, by the followers of the religion, for this new body. When found, the new individual becomes the Dalai Lama and so the cycle continues.

Models of loss

There are several models that have been suggested to explain and to understand the mourning process, some of which will be referred to later in the text.

Mourning, as mentioned earlier, tends to follow a pattern, whether the loss relates to a lost object or to the death of a person. Obviously the intensity and impact of the losses will be very different, but the general stages and reactions are the same.

If we look at a very simple model of loss, such as the loss of a favourite book, we can see the general pattern of reaction over a period of time. This can actually help us in following and understanding the process of greater losses and mourning.

You should now stop reading and consider your likely reactions to being unable to find a favourite book. Consider your first reaction and the feelings it brings. Now, consider how you might feel about the loss after a week, then a month and finally a year, after the book has been lost. Write down your thoughts for each of the time periods and compare them to the model of loss shown below.

Mourning for a lost book

A general model of bereavement is shown in Table 1a below, demonstrating the process through which an individual will pass during a period of mourning.

Table 1a: Reaction to loss: General model

Loss → Shock → Searching → Anger → Depression → Resolution
      Disbelief   Annoyance   Guilt   Denial

The first reaction to the loss of a favourite book is likely to be shock and disbelief. We cannot accept that the book has disappeared and that we can't find it in its usual, safe place. This shock and disbelief will change as we begin to search for the book, perhaps at quite a frenetic pace at first. We just 'know' that the book has to be here somewhere and are determined to find it. Later, when we still haven't found the book, our feelings will turn to anger and annoyance at our failure to easily locate it. We may also start to apportion blame, such as someone else must have moved the book and has not returned it to its proper place. This may, or may not, be realistic, depending on the circumstances. We may also think, every now and then, that we have at last found the missing book, only to realise that we have made a mistake and merely found another, similar-looking book.

Our anger may not be sustained over too lengthy a period, and is likely to be replaced by despair and depression as we realise that we are not going to find the book at all. There may also be an element of guilt, perhaps because the book was a gift from someone close, and regret, because we should have taken better care of it. We wish we could have a second chance, then we would, of course, treat the cherished book in a far better way than before and make provision for its safe keeping. We may make a sort of 'bargaining prayer' for its return on these conditions. Eventually, over time, we will be able to tolerate the loss of the book. We have resolved and accepted the reality of the loss and come to terms with the fact that it is no longer in our life. We will probably give up looking for the book and spend less time thinking about it. Certain encounters may make us remember the book, such as if we wish to refer to it for some reason, but generally we have now accepted that it is gone.

As a model of loss, this is rigid and over-simplifies matters, but it does give a basic guideline. The bereaved will not necessarily follow a straight path during the grieving for their loss, but may 'jump' from one stage to another, back and forth. This will occur over a lengthy period of time until the final resolution and acceptance of the loss is accomplished.

Mourning for a person

So, the loss of a favourite book, however special, cannot be compared to the loss of an individual, although there are elements which in principle are similar.

Tatelbaum (1990) describes the grief process as involving the initial grief experience which is later followed by both recovery and final resolution. This integration of a loss into our life may take any period of time, depending on the circumstances surrounding the loss, the nature of the attachment and our own previous life experiences.

Kubler-Ross (1982) postulated a stage-based mourning process, based on research with terminally ill patients. In other words, the bereaved passes through a series of stages, from initial shock to final resolution. The time period of the various stages will again depend on the individual, the relationship and attachment bond and the circumstances of the death.

Shock, disbelief and denial

The bereft individual may first go through a stage of feeling shocked, accompanied by numbness, confusion and disbelief, when first hearing news of a death. The fact that the death, although accepted on one level, may not be fully internalised can lead to a period of denial, during which the bereft may both act and behave as if the deceased is still alive. This may be expressed through a range of actions such as laying a place for the deceased at meal times, talking about them as if they are going to return, continuing to wash and iron their clothes, etc. The bereaved may also have difficulty with sleeping, neglecting to take proper care of themselves or the home and children. Alternatively the bereaved may exhibit compulsive behaviour, keeping the house spotless and becoming meticulous in everything they do. This can often be a distracting technique which keeps their mind off the reality of what has happened.

Despair, anguish, fear and searching

This will be followed by a period of despair, even anguish, and the bereaved may feel quite lonely and isolated. They may experience panic attacks and feel that they cannot cope without the deceased. There can be a period of literally searching for the deceased, revisiting old 'stamping grounds' where they spent time together, especially those with happy memories attached. The bereft may also feel the need to return to the place where the death occurred, either a hospital, accident site or work place. After the funeral this may include the grave or place where the ashes were scattered.

Sometimes the bereaved may think they have caught sight of the deceased, in the street or on a bus. On one level they are expecting to see the deceased, hoping that everything will return to normal, or that they will be able to say the things they did not have the opportunity to before the death. When they catch a glimpse of someone wearing familiar clothes or who is perhaps of a similar size and build, they are naturally reminded of the deceased. The reaction of disappointment can be great when they realise that in fact it is a total stranger.

Sometimes the bereft may literally seek the deceased through a medium, or through their own dreams. They may 'feel' the presence of the deceased, and in the case of sensory hallucination may even smell and hear the deceased. Parkes (1987) found in research that around 50% of widows still had very vivid dreams about their dead partners and thought that they had 'sensed' them, some time after the death.

The bereaved may cling to artefacts previously owned by the deceased, which become quite treasured possessions. This is quite normal within reasonable limits, though some may become obsessive, keeping rooms exactly as they were on the day of the death and so on.

Guilt and anger

Feelings of guilt and anger may predominate at these times, as may thoughts of what they could, or should, have done. The bereaved may also dwell on what they would do differently if they were given a second chance. Bereaved individuals can be very harsh judges of themselves, believing that if only they had done something differently the death would never have happened. Generally their views are unrealistic, as they will have done everything anyone would have expected of them in the circumstances.

The bereaved may hope that it has all been a dream and that they will eventually wake up from this vivid nightmare. They may make a 'bargaining prayer' that they will behave much better if it all really is a dream and they can have the deceased returned to them. There may also be some feelings of anger towards the deceased for having 'deserted' them, leaving them behind to cope alone. This is especially likely to happen if the death was very sudden and without warning.

Often the bereaved can feel resentful of those around them, who have not suffered and whose 'lot' in life seems so much better. This can be especially true around times such as Christmas, when everyone is caught up in family celebrations and living life to the full. Such times are harsh reminders of the loss of the future with the deceased, and happy times that 'might have been'.

Another aspect, concerning religion, is that the bereaved may start having doubts about their own faith. They may, for example, wonder how a God in whom they held such strong beliefs, could let such a terrible thing happen. How, if such unfair things happen, can there be a God? Others may find great strength from their beliefs in which case this is not an issue. Bornstein et al (1973) found some evidence suggesting that religious faith provides at least some sort of inoculation against the extremes of grief. In this study, those widows attending church on a regular basis had far less post-bereavement problems.

The bereaved may show signs of anger towards those who they perceive, correctly or not, to be responsible for the death of their loved one. This anger may be directed at the professionals involved, such as a medical team, ambulance crew or police team attending the accident, or at individuals who were present. The bereaved may feel that had these people responded more quickly or acted differently in the circumstances, the death could have been prevented. In reality this anger will not change anything, though it must be worked through slowly to reach a final resolution.

Depression, withdrawal and isolation

This stage of anger may be followed by periods of depression and withdrawal. The bereft may see no future in continuing with life and become withdrawn from society, friends and relatives. There may even be thoughts of suicide at this time, as they perceive that life isn't worth living any more and they can't cope alone. Indeed, studies have shown that the partner of a deceased individual is at a higher risk of themselves dying during the period of their bereavement.

With this withdrawal from society, there may also come a period of isolation, as friends and relatives despair in attempting to persuade the bereaved to 'pick up their life again'. The bereaved may lose their support network, as their friends and relatives lose patience and stop trying to help and support. This will only compound the problem as the bereaved becomes more isolated and withdrawn.

Resolution

This is the final stage of the mourning process, a concluding resolution of the loss, in that the bereaved will now come to terms with what has happened and see a future. The deceased still remains in the memory, but the life of the bereaved can now continue without the loss being so dominating or such a large preoccupation in their life. It is at this point that the period of mourning is completed.

The bereaved may become more involved in society and may even think in terms of other relationships, a notion which is strongly rejected during the earlier stages of mourning. There is always the danger of entering into a new relationship too quickly at this vulnerable time, perhaps for all the wrong reasons, such as to avoid loneliness. Many organisations, such as Cruse, often organise social groups to help with this difficult area.

The length of mourning

This whole process may take place over quite a lengthy period of time. Two years is often considered to be an average length of time to work through the whole process of mourning, but there will obviously be wide variations within this average time period. Children, and indeed some adults, may need additional help in order to successfully come to terms with their feelings and to connect these feelings with their loss. All the feelings such as guilt, anger, depression and despair may need to be worked through in therapy or counselling, in order for the mourning process to be successfully resolved. If the bereft individual was actually witness to the death, perhaps in an accident or major disaster, specialist help will be needed for syndromes such as post traumatic stress disorder or survivor guilt syndrome. Post traumatic stress disorder was highlighted after the Vietnam war, when many of the combatants who had experienced combat and trauma of a high level were psychologically affected. Areas such as this are highly specialised and beyond the scope of this book, but there are specialist organisations which can provide the relevant help.

The intensity of grief may well vary over time and the stages will not necessarily follow a predictable, theoretical pattern. Parkes (1986), in a study of London widows in their first year of bereavement, brought forward the notion of the fluidity of grieving. In essence, the bereaved goes through some, or even all, of the previously mentioned stages of grief but not necessarily in a fixed or rigid order. Although bereaved individuals often experience similar reactions, the individual is not on a fixed trajectory and can return to an 'earlier' stage of grieving.

The intensity of grieving may well vary during a weekly cycle, especially for those in employment. The weekend, for example, may present a harder time for the bereaved than weekdays. Those at work, where they fit in to some sort of routine normality, can endure these days assuming they did not work with the deceased. During the working week there is at least a continuation of a fixed pattern, whilst the unstructured weekends may cause problems as the bereaved may feel quite lost in the absence of the deceased. Most people, especially those who have not been through a relatively recent period of mourning themselves, may tend to consider a two year period of mourning beyond that which is considered reasonable. Those individuals not having experienced a recent bereavement may well wonder why the bereft is still not 'over' the death after a matter of weeks, and may expect everything to return to normal far sooner than the actual time to final resolution takes. This expectation may itself compound the problem, as the bereft may find no sympathetic ear in their immediate social circle. Again, this can lead to withdrawal and the potential for the bereaved to find themselves in isolation. Anniversaries and other special occasions, such as Christmas and birthdays, also present a range of problems. The first anniversary of the death may be a time when events of the previous years flood back in the mind and are relived intensely by the bereaved. The arrival of birthdays can bring memories of previous, happier times, when the bereaved may dwell on thoughts of what might have been but for the loss of their loved one. These times bring mourning for the loss of a future. Issues of both regret and possibly guilt may then again be raised in the mind of the bereaved.

As already mentioned, both the intensity and length of time of the mourning process will depend on a variety of factors. These include the strength of the bond between the bereaved and the deceased, the circumstances of the death and the previous experiences of loss of the bereaved. It is in this latter area of bereavement which teachers can effectively address issues and help children through pro-active strategies. Ideally this should be well before the child has experienced any large and traumatic loss in their life.

Tasks of mourning

Another model of grieving was proposed by Worden (1984), who saw the bereaved as having to complete certain tasks of mourning before they could eventually reach the resolution stage of their loss. These tasks, as shown in Table 1b, are firstly to accept the reality of the loss and secondly to fully experience the pain of the grief. The third task is to adjust to a new environment and finally to begin investing in new relationships. It is suggested that the bereaved individual needs to go through, and complete, each of these tasks, in order to enable them to fully complete the mourning process. In this model, the bereaved is far more active than passive, and in terms of counselling can be helped to gradually work through the tasks, step by step.

In this model, resolution of the mourning process is completed when the bereaved transfer their energy from the deceased and invest it elsewhere. This means that while the deceased will remain in the memory of the bereaved, they do not dominate their thoughts and actions and they are able to move on.

> **Table 1b: The tasks of mourning**
>
> To accept the reality of loss.
> To experience the pain of grief.
> To adjust to a new environment.
> To invest in new relationships.

Previous experience of loss

One factor in our ability to cope with a bereavement seems to be our previous experiences and strategies which we have developed in coping with some of the smaller losses in life. It seems that those children who have already coped successfully with some of these little losses, such as a brief separation from their parents or the death of a family pet, are likely to be better prepared for a major loss than those who have been shielded from the effects of loss by well-meaning adults. It has been claimed that a failure to deal properly with these little losses in childhood can result in problems later in life. These problems may include a greater need for psychiatric help, proneness to depression and also a failure to deal with other losses that the individual may encounter in their adult life. This is therefore an issue of great importance in relation to children, in that preventative measures can be taken to help them avoid, or at least minimise, such problems in later life.

The balance of the family

The family is a system, and although human relationships are dynamic, there is likely to be some sort of equilibrium and balance in the family system.

The death of a family member will throw the whole system out of balance, into disequilibrium. One perspective of the period of mourning, at this level, is the time taken for the system to readjust and then gradually return to a new equilibrium. The situation is not dissimilar from that of an individual leaving the family home for other reasons, such as divorce, separation or going to college. In all of these cases the family system is thrown out of equilibrium and needs time to find a new level and a new balance.

If one parent dies, it may be that some of the roles previously carried out by the deceased are taken over by another member of the family. In the case of young parents and family, the role is likely to be taken up by the surviving parent, but it could be that either a friend or a relation steps into the breach. If the parent is unable to pass over some of these roles, then this may impose further stresses and strains on the family. Some of these roles, perhaps defined as less essential, may be either abandoned or amended, to suit the new family structure. If there are older children in the family, then they may be expected to take on more responsibility, taking on some of the roles of the deceased parent. An older child may, for example, become more involved in caring for the younger family members or housework. Responsibility may be thrust, perhaps even unreasonably, onto other family members, representing another loss in terms of freedom for these children who are being expected to grow up more quickly. Any disturbance of the balance is likely to have implications for all the family members. The siblings may initially feel quite lonely if a brother or sister has died, or may worry that a similar fate will befall them or remaining members of their family. However, in the medium term it is likely that some form of equilibrium will be restored to the effectively functioning family system.

The balance above the family level

There are potentially levels of mourning and imbalance after a death which are far beyond that of just the immediate family, depending on the role and status of the deceased.

At one extreme, the death of a head of state could well cause an imbalance at a national level, depending on general stability. An imbalance of the higher echelons of state could well result in the creation of a power vacuum, which could perhaps be followed by a coup and a change of the party running a country. There could also be both nationally based mourning and national ceremonies of rights of passage, which are not really for the benefit of the deceased or their immediate family but serve as a public acknowledgement. The ceremonies may include those relating to the transfer of power, in effect for the benefit of the new person now assuming the recently vacated role, such as a coronation, focusing on the continuity element of power. In these circumstances, the immediate family may well have to set aside their own grieving and follow the formal, national rituals.

There may be a similar process at the time of a national disaster, when the attention of a nation is focused on the mourning and national commemorations take place.

Below the extremes of the death of a state leader or national disaster, there will be people or events of regional or local significance which will need to be acknowledged at a public level. These may include an horrific accident, murder or similar disaster in a local community, causing a regional imbalance and a period of community mourning.

This will especially be the case in the event of an untimely death, or death involving children, particularly if large numbers are killed in one incident. Initially there will be shock and disbelief concerning what has happened and the early local reaction. Sometimes public grieving is shown by the laying of flowers at the scene of a fatal accident and by local services of remembrance. There is likely to be intense media attention, particularly at the local level.

If trauma has taken place, perhaps an horrific accident involving young children, then the local community may also exhibit a trauma reaction. Individuals, especially children, may develop irrational fears that the event may reoccur. An atmosphere of communal hysteria may even emerge, in which case the authorities will need to respond.

On an individual level, those involved may require further help through counselling or therapy, to help them recover from the ordeal of trauma. Many local authorities now plan a pro-active response to such local disasters, by preparing teams of counsellors able to provide immediate support in a time of need. These teams can respond quickly, for example, attending a school to help if there has been a traumatic incident involving some of the pupils.

The grieving model can be equally applied to local communities or countries, as it can to individuals and families. There will be differences in both intensity and length of grieving after such incidents, but the grieving of close family members will obviously take a lot longer than the general members of the community.

Communities too can be traumatised by particular horrific events and may need help to resolve matters, such as coming to terms with what has happened or feelings of survivor guilt. Often communities react in both a positive and a united way after the initial shock of a disaster. This happened with the community of Locherbie, after the bombed aircraft crashed from the sky.

Individuals also tend to unite in adversity, such as when fighting in combat, or in other war-type situations. Another example is the 'Blitz' in London, during the second world war, where the community responded positively despite the horrific devastation.

Often the community will be mobilised quickly and volunteers will come forward to help.

The restoration of a community equilibrium can take place relatively quickly, depending on the circumstances. This contrasts with the immediate family of the deceased, as their own personal mourning will proceed over a far longer period.

Follow-up Activities

1. Recall losing a much favoured object. Can you remember both your initial and subsequent feelings, as you realised that it was not going to be found?
2. Do you have negative feelings about the subject of death? If so, can you think of the reasons for this?
3. Is it easier to discuss death with a close relative, close friend or complete stranger? If there is a difference, can you think of a reason why?
4. Think of a special object or souvenir that you have. Why is it so special to you?

CHAPTER 3

Death and Children

It is unrealistic to assume that most children have not encountered 'second-hand', media-type death from a relatively young age. Television is a favourite pastime for many children and they will most likely have observed fictional death on the television. Children may also have incorporated death into their games, such as doctors and nurses, 'bang-bang, you're dead' and 'zapping' type games. Children will mimic the adult world, both what they see via the media and in their day to day lives. They often play 'mums and dads', have pretend tea parties with their toys and dress up.

Through their many games it seems, even if perhaps superficially in the context of play, that they are relatively comfortable with many 'adult' concepts, including death. This is, however, a 'second hand' experience of death.

Children are also likely to have encountered death in other areas of their life. For example, dead animals they may see on shopping trips, perhaps during a trip to the supermarket, meat prepared in the kitchen at home, etc. Children are likely to be familiar with these animals in their live states as well as in the form we buy them for food.

It may be that children growing up in rural areas encounter 'first-hand' death in their environment, being closer to nature and food production. They are more likely to be aware that animals are reared and killed for meat production, as this is part of their daily lives.

Children's concept of death

Quite young children seem to acquire at least some notion of the concept of death. This concept may be muddled and formed through daily experiences such as the media, games and playground conversations. In many ways this mirrors the way children acquire their early knowledge regarding many 'adult issues', such as sexual matters.

Adults may underestimate not only what children understand about death, but also the potential ability of children to cope and deal with bereavement, given optimum conditions. It seems reasonable to assume that, as with sex, children gradually accumulate knowledge in the area of death, until with age and experience they acquire an adult concept of death. However, the information they gather may be acquired through inappropriate sources, including myths and half truths from their siblings or peers. Unfortunately, while children may receive clarification of the facts regarding sex matters, through carefully targeted education at school and from parents, there seems to be little provision for direct education of children in the area of death. Nagy was one of the first researchers to study children and the concept of death, reported by Kastenbaum and Aisenberg (1972). Other research, such as by Zach (1978) indicated that even by the time children reach early school age, the average child has already begun to grasp both the meaning and fear of death. It is unlikely that young babies will have any concept of loss through death, though they may gradually become more aware of absences, and of changes in the people around caring for them. Children under three years of age will be unlikely to understand death, but they will probably understand and perhaps fear separation from their siblings or peers. The same may well apply to other separations, such as through divorce, a parent working away from home, or the admission of a parent to hospital. Children of a slightly older age will be far more aware of the person mainly caring for them and will therefore be far more aware of any changes in this relationship. In the case of a death, these children need to have their routines maintained as much as possible. They may be starting to grasp the concept of death but are unlikely to regard it as a permanent state. They may perceive death to be similar to sleep or a journey, a state from which the individual will eventually return. This idea may well be supported in television programmes as cartoon characters recover quickly from violent deaths, and so on.

Children at this age will also be starting to ask 'Why?' questions to everything they see around them. This presents parents with an ideal opportunity to discuss death with the child, at the child's level of understanding, and in a natural, unthreatening environment.

Kane (1979) also helped to provide further evidence in this area. The Kane study suggested that children do gradually build up a concept of death, and that as their understanding changes and develops at different ages, they finally adopt an adult concept of death.

Children as young as three will have gained a realisation of death, although it is not until the average child reaches the age of six that they will fully comprehend that death is irreversible.

A later study by Lansdown and Benjamin (1985), indicated an even greater understanding of death by young children. In this study, about a third of five-year-old children had a good concept of death, including the concept that the deceased cannot return. However, many children do not fully grasp the concept and may still wonder how the deceased feed or go to the toilet.

Older children will have grasped some more complex, conceptual understanding of death but may still think of death literally, in terms of death being a person. At this older age, children may perceive death in terms of it happening to an unlucky person or a bad person. They may also associate death with violence or trauma, such as in an accident or by murder. This is again a reflection of the amount of media death which they observe on a daily basis.

Children will probably not achieve a truly adult concept of death until they reach the age of twelve, although there will of course be wide variations depending on the maturity and experiences of the individual. Table 2 gives a general guide to the likely understanding of children and young people, regarding the concept of death.

Table 2: Children and the concept of death

Baby:	No concept of death: loss of carer.
Infant age:	Notion of death, though seen as a reversible state.
Junior age:	Concept of death developing, though some strange ideas.
Secondary age:	An adult concept of death.

In contrast to younger children, older children may well become quite fearful of death, perhaps relating to the lack details and information made available to them. This dearth of knowledge is a reflection of our cultural taboo of the subject. By the time children reach secondary school age, most of them will have developed a full and adult understanding of death.

However well prepared, a bereavement will be a traumatic event for any child, as the security of their world is threatened. For the adolescent, a bereavement may be especially difficult, coming at a time when they are also experiencing other difficulties and changes. The adolescent will be coping with many other issues in their life, such as the loss of childhood, gaining of independence and the physical and emotional changes associated with puberty.

The child does not have the adult benefits of experience of life and maturity, and may have problems in understanding the implications of a death, beyond the immediate loss. The comprehension of some children, for example those with learning difficulties, may lag behind the norms for their peer group. In addition, some children may well be more precocious and have a far more mature understanding of death than would be expected.

Adults, children and death

Adults may generally feel very uncomfortable in talking with other adults about the subject of death and are likely to find that broaching the topic with children is even more difficult. It may be easier for many adults to simply avoid the subject rather than risk a problematic interaction with the children. Adults may consider, perhaps wrongly, that children are not fully able to understand death and that they would find it far too difficult to cope with the subject. Pattison (1976) claimed that many of the problems which families have in coping with death centres around the contemporary issue that death today is a taboo subject. Evidence does seem to suggest that children can potentially cope with the area of death, though to achieve this they do need to be provided both with adequate knowledge and experiences. Children seem to have far more knowledge and a greater awareness of death than most adults believe.

How death is different for children: information and control

Although children do still follow the same general pattern of adult grief and mourning, there are ways in which their experiences of death and bereavement will diverge from that of the adult. Although children may have some general understanding of death, they may well lack the factual information concerning what is happening in a given situation. Children may be the last ones to be told what is happening in a crisis, if they are told at all. One reason why knowledge is not transferred immediately may be because the adults are in a state of shock and are preoccupied with their own state.

Children are also likely to have far less control over the general circumstances than adults in the same position. The children may not be able to initiate enquiries about what is happening, although they can sense that all is not well. For example, in a hospital waiting room after an accident or difficult operation.

It is these areas of control and access to information that separate children's experience of death from that of the adults involved. Children need to have things carefully explained to them, both in a sympathetic and sensitive manner.

There is a natural tendency for adults to try and protect children from certain experiences, but with the area of death this protection may not be effective other than in the short term.

In the situation of encountering death, adults may themselves be uncertain as to exactly what is happening and may themselves feel frightened and bewildered. If this is the case, then the needs of the children may easily be overlooked.

It is also important that any children involved are not left with strangers at such times of crisis, but that they have an immediate link with someone whom they know and trust. If this is not possible, then they should at least be given as much constancy and continuity in the provision of temporary care as is possible in the circumstances.

Fear of others in the family dying

The death of a major figure, such as a parent, is likely to make a child feel insecure and to fear that others in their family may also die. The child can feel that their whole 'world' is collapsing and that it will continue to do so. If a sibling has died, then the child may fear that they will be next, especially if they are younger. In these circumstances, the child may be particularly fearful when they reach the age at which their sibling died.

This insecurity and fear needs to be addressed and it is necessary for the adults around to reassure the child. Adults may need reassurance themselves, but are far more able to rationalise matters through their wider experience of life, even if they are not totally able to eliminate their fears. Children lack this experience and therefore may have their fears compounded. Table 3 provides a summary of the possible experiences children may have during a bereavement.

Table 3: The child's experience of death	
The child may lack:	**The child may then:**
1. Understanding. 2. Facts. 3. Control.	1. Fear the worst. 2. Fear that other family members may die. 3. Insecurity and over-protectiveness. Feel alone and isolated with their fears.

The reactions of children to news of a death

Sometimes children seem able to compartmentalize bereavement, separating it out from the rest of their life, so that they don't show the typical adult reactions. Young children, for example, may be very upset when they are first told of a death, or they may show no reaction at all and carry on as if nothing has happened.

It is as if children need to absorb the fact of the bereavement and grief gradually and here they may need help to accept the reality of the death. Bending (1993) gave examples of children showing what seemed to be complete indifference to the news of death, for example a teenager going out to a party after hearing that his father had died, or a younger child going out to play with her friends.

Bending sees this apparent indifference as children concealing the grief that they really feel inside. Perhaps because the news is too much to assimilate at once, the child adopts this strategy in order to cope. With regard to a death which is not so sudden and unexpected, such as a long term illness where some sort of planning can be involved, Kubler-Ross (1982) emphasised the need for the adults and children involved to share feelings and concerns both before and after the event. Here, children should be directly involved, as far as is appropriate in the given circumstances.

Regression

Children affected by a bereavement may yearn for an earlier, and seemingly more secure time. It may be that some regressive behaviour occurs and that the children exhibit the behaviour appropriate from this past 'golden age'. These signs of regression include bed-wetting, thumb sucking, developing a fear of the dark and needing the light to be kept on at night, and so on. Regression may also be displayed in a more physical manner, such as developing the need to cuddle a previously discarded toy or sleeping with a favourite blanket. The child's insecurity may also be reflected in them suddenly developing separation anxiety, with them becoming very unwilling to go out and join in with friends in their usual play. This 'clinging' behaviour is again representative of needing a previous, more secure age, though may also relate to the fear that if they leave the family home another family member may die.

Magical powers and guilt

If the child is at the egocentric stage of development, that is around the infant age, there is a danger that the child may perceive that they themselves caused the death, through their own self-ascribed 'magical powers'. The child may, for example, have said in the heat of an argument, that they wished the deceased was dead. This has the potential to generate feelings of guilt, as the child may connect these two events, their wish and the subsequent death, and assume that these events are linked. Black (1993) describes working with a child still convinced, three years after the death of her mother, that something she had said in the middle of a row had actually caused the death.

Involvement of children after a death

When a close family member is dying or has died, the children may well be 'farmed out' to neighbours or relations during the crisis period. In reality the children may prefer, and may well be more secure, to stay at the family home remaining in contact with familiar things. By remaining at home, children are able to build up their own learning experiences, their knowledge and their coping strategies, with the support and guidance of the adults around them. Children, especially those sent away at a time of crisis, may well be given only limited information about what is happening. They may even be given misleading reassurance from the adults around them, indicating that all is really well, when in fact the opposite is the case. In such circumstances, children are likely to fantasize about what is happening and their fears may begin to exceed the reality of the situation. It is far better that adults are honest with them from the start and that the family openly share the experience, as appropriate.

It may be useful for the children to keep, or have access to, something which belonged to the deceased, as a reminder and keepsake during this initial period and later.

Protection of children

When a crisis occurs in a family the news of what is actually happening, or has already happened, will eventually 'leak out' to the children. This may be through overhearing adults talk or through their peers in the playground. This in itself can cause a temporary damage to the adult-child relationship, as the child feels the adult can no longer be trusted. It is the typical 'Father Christmas syndrome', where the child is being taught a lesson that adults pretend and cannot always be trusted in some matters of great importance.

Parents often seem to create a 'fairytale' world for their children, in which everything is safe, stable and cosy. While this is done with all the best intentions, it can make some of 'life's lessons' much harder for their children in the long run. At some point they are going to have to deal with reality and understand that there is an unfair and unkind world outside the family unit.

Death is one of the areas from which parents may try to protect their children, through such tactics as avoiding the topic altogether, or withholding important information from the children. Leshan (1979) contended that children should be told the truth and should be allowed to share their feelings of grief with the family adults around them. It can be claimed that it is in their long term interest that young children are not totally protected from the reality of death, since they will eventually become adults themselves and have to deal with losses, deaths and bereavements. Adults should also not be afraid to outwardly show their grief. This grief should be shared by all the family and seen as a natural and healing process. Berry (1991) showed how even quite young children can become actively involved after the death of a sibling or parent, given a sensitive and caring approach.

In research, many adults relate to problems which they experience later in life, which can be directly linked with times in their childhood where their parents have handled a death situation very badly. Such problems can be created by parents 'pretending' to the children that nothing has happened for them to be worried about, not sharing the truth to a level which the children understand or excluding the children completely from the mourning process. The effects of some parents' actions may not only inhibit, but also distort, the natural grieving process of a child. This can cause many short term problems, which may in turn lead to long term problems such as an extremely late resolution of grief. Children are essentially no different from adults in that they have their own grief reactions to losses and bereavements, and also in having the need to work through the processes of grieving and mourning to the eventual and final resolution of their grief.

Where practical and possible, children should not be excluded when a death occurs. They should be allowed the opportunity to become actively involved in the mourning process, relating to their special person, if that is what they wish. They should always have choice and should never be forced to do something against their will. Depending on the age of the children involved, they should be allowed to choose whether or not to view the body, whether they attend the funeral, etc. In most cases, attending the funeral will help the child, assuming that they are of an appropriate age to work through the first two Worden tasks of mourning. Even if they do not feel able to attend the funeral, the children may still want to be involved in other arrangements. Adults should discuss options, such as helping with the food for the mourners, or writing a farewell letter to be buried with the deceased, as appropriate.

If the children, after consideration, do decide to attend the funeral, or to view the body of the deceased, having had no previous experiences of this nature, it is important that a close and trusted adult gives them some idea of what they can expect in preparation for either event.

Table 4 summarises some of the reactions which children may exhibit after a bereavement.

Table 4: Some reactions which children may exhibit after a death

Regression

Feelings of guilt

Exclusion

Protective towards siblings or parents

Delayed or inhibited mourning

The need to grieve and be involved

Isolation, protection and fantasies

The bereaved adult may feel and become very isolated, having nobody with whom they can talk, confide in and share their loss. This may well be the case relatively shortly after the funeral, when many will assume that the bereaved person has 'got over' the death and are 'pulling themselves together'. There may also be additional problems for the bereaved adult to face, such as financial difficulties and a reduced standard of living or status.

Any children involved may also become isolated and be compounded by the lack of information from the remaining parent about what is going to happen next. There are a variety of situations in which the child will feel unable to ask relevant questions, whether through fear of hearing the worst or of further upsetting the adults around them. The child may be seeking to protect the adults, as the adults are similarly shielding the child. Children will, however, detect an atmosphere of tension prevailing in the home, despite any attempts the adults may make to give the opposite impression. Children are extremely sensitive to change and although they may not be aware of the causes, they will know that something is amiss. By not talking to the children, there is a risk that they will begin to imagine what is happening, and their imaginations can make a situation far worse than the reality. Their fantasies can often fill them with fear and lead to further avoidance in seeking the truth. These problems are avoidable if the children are kept fully informed, within the limits of their understanding. The information given to the children should be at the level of their own maturity and understanding. The technical details should be avoided, such as complex medical terminology or graphic details of an accident scene, which children will not fully comprehend and may 'take away' to worry about further. It is far better to give the child a short simple explanation to which they can easily relate, such as that a particular part of the body has simply 'worn out'. In general, of course, the older the child the greater their ability to understand, in which case more details can be shared.

Euphemisms

Euphemisms tend to arise around any taboo subject and are a way of addressing the area indirectly, rather than using a straight approach. There are a variety of euphemisms surrounding the area of death, some of which are listed in Table 5. All of these euphemisms can have a very negative potential in relation to children, and as such they should be carefully avoided. Children, especially those of a young age, are likely to take euphemisms literally and this can lead to serious problems. For example, the child may worry that they too will 'go to sleep' and not wake up, in which case they may avoid bedtime and be too frightened to sleep at night in case they die. They may also fear that they will be 'lost' or 'taken by Jesus', in which case they will become very 'clingy' and perhaps suffer panic attacks at the thought of leaving the safety of the home.

It is far better that the children are told the truth in terms they can understand, although as already mentioned, this must be in the limits of the children's maturity and understanding.

Whatever the child is told, it should be linked with any previous, similar experiences and explained within their conceptual understanding of death. Children should never be misled or told lies.

Table 5: Euphemisms for death

Gone to sleep

Lost

Crossed over to the other side

Passed over

Climbed the ladder to heaven

Taken by Jesus

Kicked the bucket

Children and death at school

It is very useful for teachers to have a general awareness of the grief process. This knowledge will help both the teachers and other staff at the school to recognise, understand and cope with the changes that may take place in the behaviour of a child after a bereavement. It will help in developing an empathy with the child.

Post bereavement changes may affect the child's behaviour, or their academic performance at school, or even both of these. Children may be affected even after quite a lengthy period of time following the bereavement, after it has perhaps been assumed that they have fully recovered. At school, the child may be going through any of the stages of bereavement, from initially being in a state of shock or disbelief, to displaying anger, frustration or guilt, to being withdrawn and isolating themselves from others.

They may be preoccupied at times, producing little work or displaying aggressive behaviour towards other members of the class. In Humberside, the studies by Holland (1993) and Holland and Ludford (1995) revealed that teachers noticed all of the stages bereavement in bereft children at school, as shown in Table 6.

Table 6: Things teachers noticed at school, in bereft children

Anger
Frustration
Withdrawal
Lethargy
Depression

The context of school in society

Schools are an established, institutionalised part of society and as such are not immune from the effects of death being generally perceived in our culture as taboo. Teachers, and other staff in schools, may themselves have had problems and difficulties with a number of losses in their lives, including death. Many may generally be uncomfortable with the subject of death and may have their own negative perceptions concerning the topic. They may hold unfavourable attitudes and adverse experiences of their own, especially if they themselves have been bereaved and have not yet fully resolved their loss. Even if this attitude is not articulated, it may be expressed in the form of non-verbal communication. Non-verbal communication comprises a large proportion of total communication between individuals and as such is an important element of interaction, either conforming or conflicting with verbal messages.

Even very young children can be very astute at identifying non-verbal clues and will find it difficult to discuss any of their own concerns with a teacher if they perceive a poor reception is likely.

It is strange that while most children will receive clarification of sexual issues and processes through a carefully targeted education, there seems to be very little provision for the same in the area of death.

There are great benefits to be gained by children if the school does adopt a positive approach to the area of loss and bereavement. During term time, the children will spend a large proportion of their days at school, and in a sense the school may well be their potentially secure, second family. This may be even more so in the case of a family loss, where the other family members may be so involved in coping with their own problems and grief, that school is the only stable, safe haven to the child. At school, patterns, habits and daily routines can be maintained, providing a valuable, secure setting for the children for a proportion of their day.

The children's daily routines at home may have been greatly disturbed around the time of the death, and they may change in the long term as a new family equilibrium is formed. The potential of schools to provide a safe haven in these circumstances was mentioned by Adams (1992) in a young person's account of bereavement and how it is not effectively addressed in schools or colleges.

Greater knowledge and awareness by teachers will help to maximise the potential benefits which the school can provide and create in helping to support the bereaved child in these circumstances.

Follow-up Activities

1. Can you remember what you were told about death as a young child? What was your first source of information?
2. What can you recall about the first funeral you attended? How old were you? Was it what you had expected and what were your feelings?
3. If you have attended a funeral more recently, in which ways was the experience different and in which the same?
4. Which television programme have you most recently enjoyed and why?

Part Two: The Pro-active Approach

One of the most important factors in the area of support for the bereaved child, is the establishment of good, long term relations between the school and home, as well as between the school staff and parents. Schools should ideally be perceived by parents as part of the local community and not just as an educational outpost. Hopefully, in the right circumstances, the parents will support the school, which in turn sets the foundations for maintaining a flow of information between the home and school, both formal and informal.

Links between home and school should be fostered, avoiding any dominance by small cliches. Good links with the home will foster and develop mutual trust and sharing between parents and teachers. This can be started immediately when children begin at the school and need support through the potential crisis of leaving the family unit, perhaps for the first time. A process of induction involving the parents, teachers and children can be very important. Teachers are important role models, especially at times of crisis, and how they react will be noticed by the children as well as their parents.

Schools can support a bereaved child in two specific ways as shown in Table 7. Initially, and ideally, schools need to be able to react quickly and positively to an emergency situation, such as a death. The teachers and other staff should also be able to support the child through the bereavement, not only when the death occurs but also for however long it takes for the child to resolve their grief. This support is a re-active process, and there should ideally be a planned, pro-active element in place to respond to a bereavement. Planning is crucial in order to avoid crisis management at the time a bereavement occurs. The school staff may themselves be in a state of shock and be going through the grief and mourning processes, and without a set of guidelines already in place they are unlikely to respond appropriately.

Things should not be left to chance and schools' staff should at least have the knowledge to know where to find further, professional help and support when needed.

The second way in which schools can help children in the areas of death and bereavement, is by adopting a pro-active approach and addressing the area of loss through the curriculum. In this way, the curriculum can be used to help improve the long term prospects of the children in relation to their understanding of, and responses to, death and losses in general. One factor, already mentioned, in our ability to cope with a bereavement is our previous experiences, both positive and negative, and not just losses relating to bereavement.

The curriculum already includes processes of life, such as sexuality, childbirth, life cycles, etc., and yet the one great certainty of life, death, is not fully addressed.

Not only can the development and implementation of a pro-active approach help the children to reach a greater understanding of death and loss, but it should also hopefully enable children to achieve better coping mechanisms in preparation for their own inevitable losses later in life.

Table 7: Two ways in which schools can help

1. Prepare children for losses they will experience in life (pro-active).
2. Help bereft children throughout a period of crisis (re-active).

CHAPTER 4

Ethos and Feelings

Loss in the curriculum

Schools can effectively help children to deal with their future losses and encounters with death, by addressing these areas in the curriculum. In this way, children can build a general framework and a better understanding of death and loss which, as we have discussed, can help them to deal with such experiences, as and when they are exposed to them.

A study in Belfast by Leckley (1991) revealed that over seventy per cent of primary school teachers thought that they had a part to play in helping children to gain an understanding of what death actually means. However, despite that defined objective, over seventy per cent of the schools in the study had no defined policy in the area of death education. The concept of loss can be presented at school, through the curriculum, in a variety of ways and some of these are described in the following text. These are ideas which can be used, amended or developed as appropriate to the circumstances of individual schools and children.

There are great opportunities for integrating the concept of loss, death and bereavement into the curriculum. The topic should be raised in both a natural and non-morose way, wherever and whenever is appropriate, without imposing any stress or anxiety on the children. Careful planning is needed with the pressure of other curriculum demands, to ensure that the areas of death and loss are not neglected but properly addressed. Once the subject has been addressed, the input should be evaluated and developed with continuity and consistency. Careful evaluation is necessary once a programme has been implemented, in order that adjustments can be made, as and when needed. This evaluation can involve teachers, other school staff and the children.

Liaison with other school staff is essential, as this will ensure an effective,

48

efficient development of the area and a whole school approach will present the best way forward.

Care must be taken whenever directly or indirectly raising the topic of bereavement and death, whether in the classroom, staffroom or planning meeting. Teachers and other staff, together with the children, may themselves have some unresolved grief and find the subject difficult, even distressing. It is essential to be aware of such issues. Hopefully, with good liaison between staff and a building of trust between the staff, parents and children, such problems can be sensitively addressed and minimised.

Assemblies

In both the primary and secondary school, assemblies provide the opportunity for the whole school ethos and culture to be reinforced and celebrated, by both staff and children. Positive events can be shared, successes and achievements rewarded and news of special occasions can be given. In addition to these positive events, sad occasions should also be shared, such as when a pupil leaves the school or if a teacher is ill or retires. If both sadness and happiness are shared together by all the staff and children, in this whole school setting, then a good example of a positive and open tone is being set for the children. Hopefully, the children will eventually internalise these proceedings and display them in their own actions.

Breaking the news

Care should be taken when breaking any bad news to the children, such as the death of a child from the school. This especially applies to those children in the younger age groups and those who had a close relationship with the deceased. These groups should be told first, in a careful and sensitive manner, by their own class teacher, before any whole school acknowledgement takes place. Most news, thankfully, is not of this nature and can be shared together, by all, from the start.

Feelings

Some children may well have difficulty with the area of feelings. These children may not be fully in touch with their own feelings and they may be unable to articulate or to express these feelings. In the area of death and bereavement children may not only be unsure of their feelings but also unable to connect their feelings with their loss. This difficulty is perhaps compounded by the traditional British culture, that is the general social expectation that we always remain stoical in adversity, never openly showing our feelings, even in the most unfavourable circumstances.

This accepted cultural norm contrasts sharply with many other cultures, including those around the Southern European area, where there may be much public showing of emotion and public venting of feelings following an event such as a tragic death or disaster. There is the danger that if we do not allow an expression of feelings, 'a vent for a volcano', then it may be manifested in other, more negative ways. This is especially true of children and may be manifested in negative changes in behaviour.

Discussions

The teacher can help children to gain an awareness of their feelings through several mediums, including that of discussion. Many teachers, especially those of the younger age groups, provide regular times, at the beginning or end of each school day, for the children to share their news with the rest of the class. These class sharing sessions do present an ideal opportunity for the children to discuss feelings and share losses, in a safe and secure setting. As they become more used to these sharing sessions they will not be afraid to share events in their life with others. It may sometimes be more appropriate for children to share with those in their own sub group and later progress to whole class discussions. The teacher should be prepared to set an example, and to share some of their own news or experiences with the class.

This time can be used to introduce the area of death and bereavement, as appropriate. The death of a class pet, for example, would provide such an opportunity for the whole class to discuss and clarify their feelings. Other examples may include when pets at home have died, when children have found an injured or dead animal in the road, the death of a major person in the local community or nationally, and so on. Teachers should acknowledge these and similar events, particularly if raised by the children, showing that they have had a significant impact. The teacher should treat these events in a natural way, as being part of life, and so encourage the children to develop a healthy attitude towards them. If the teacher changes the subject or avoids it totally, then not only is the opportunity lost to openly discuss the issue, but it may also discourage children from sharing similar things with the teacher or another adult, in the future.

Children could also be asked to talk about those things in their life which make them feel happy, in contrast to those which make them feel sad. It is important that children explore their feelings and learn to recognise them. All areas of emotion can be explored, such as anger, sadness, disappointment, worry, pride, envy, excitement and pleasure.

Some children may initially be reluctant to share in these exercises, and may be uncomfortable talking in front of their peers. The teacher can encourage these more reluctant children to join in, but they should always be treated with great sensitivity and never forced or embarrassed into taking part, until they are ready.

Listening

Implicit in discussions is the ability to listen and then respond to what is heard in an appropriate manner. During a class discussion session, only one individual can speak at one time, and the others must, by definition, listen. It is useful to establish rules beforehand, so that children know how to take turns, listen to others and wait patiently. Activities to develop listening skills are very useful and there are many books and packs available on this subject. Music lessons are an ideal opportunity for further developing listening skills, as children can listen for specific instruments which they must try and identify, or when playing instruments together must listen to each other to keep time and tune.

Writing

The expression of feelings can easily be extended to producing written work and some children may in fact find this less daunting or threatening than actually speaking directly about their feelings. The children could later be encouraged to read their written work to the rest of the class, which may be less threatening than speaking 'off the cuff'. The children could write a story describing their happiest or saddest day, or describing other feelings and emotions. They should try and relate a particular feeling to a given situation, for example falling out with a close friend, losing a family pet, going to the doctor or dentist, losing a favourite toy, receiving a surprise package in the post.

It is important, as with speaking, to include positive elements in their writing, to keep a healthy balance between the negatives and positives. Positive events may include birthdays, Christmas, winning a prize, visiting relatives, holidays, and so on. These topics should of course be related to the age, maturity and interests of the individual children.

Later, the teacher can begin to introduce more difficult concepts, relating to the children's individual experiences. These may include starting a new school, moving house, the arrival of a new baby, or sitting an examination.

A feelings book

The children may enjoy having a book in which they can write their feelings. A feelings book could be provided for each child to either write or draw their feelings, whenever they like. As an alternative, or addition, you could develop a class feelings book or graffiti board, which can be kept in the classroom for children to express their feelings at relevant times. Children may like to keep a journal or diary on a regular basis, including events both positive and negative, which they have experienced over a period of time.

Storytime

Teachers of the younger age group usually finish the school day with a story reading session. For these younger children, storytime can be used as an opportunity to raise the issue of feelings. Examples of appropriate books to initiate such discussions include, 'Dogger', by Shirley Hughes; 'The Snowman', by Raymond Briggs; and 'The Tenth Good Thing About Barney', by Judith Viorst.
'Dogger' tells of a favourite toy which goes missing and the feelings involved as the family try to retrieve the toy. In 'The Snowman' a boy builds a snowman which comes to life. They have a great adventure together and become friends, but the snowman eventually melts and the boy loses his special friend. In 'The Tenth Good Thing About Barney', a boy mourns the death of his pet cat.
All of these books provide an opportunity for the children to discuss the feelings that the characters in the book may have at various points during the story. They can also discuss how they would feel in these circumstances, or relate true stories of similar events which they have experienced. The children should be encouraged, though never forced, to share their feelings in the supportive and safe environment of the classroom.
The children may also like to share the stories that they themselves have written, during this storytime session, and then to discuss their feelings about their own stories.

Feelings and the expressive arts

Work relating to feelings can be extended beyond the areas of discussion and writing, into the general area of the arts. This can include activities such as drawing, painting, modelling, drama, mime, music and other similar art forms. Children, especially younger ones, may find it easier to express their feelings through these art forms, rather than through the more direct and restrictive approaches of talking and writing.

Facial expression and body language can also be discussed in the areas of drama and mime. In music, the children can handle various instruments and then attempt to make sounds to represent different feelings. Music presents an ideal opportunity for children to indirectly explore their feelings and they will enjoy trying to relate to their feelings through playing the instruments. They can be encouraged to compose short pieces of music reflecting a specific emotion, selecting the appropriate instruments and mood. They can also listen to pieces of music carefully selected for the purpose and try to identify which feelings the music is trying to communicate to the listener.

The use of drama presents another opportunity for the children to discuss and actually act out their feelings. This can be through the use of role play, scripted or ad lib, including a whole range of feelings. Within this area children may also use 'second hand vehicles' such as puppets, masks and costumes, which often gives them more freedom to express their feelings.

In each of these activities the children should begin by working in small, secure groups, deciding their own scenarios with limited input from the teacher. Once they have become comfortable with such activities the teacher can begin to add more direction and guide the pupils to explore more specific feelings.

Teachers may like to explore 'guided fantasy' with their class, which is a relaxation technique. The teacher relates a scenario to the children, once they are in a state of relaxation through simple meditation techniques, and takes them on an imaginary journey in their minds. There are several books available offering further details on techniques and scenarios teachers can use.

Other areas of art can be used by the children to explore feelings. They may use old magazines and newspapers to collect pictures of people showing various emotions. These may include a footballer elated at scoring a goal, a small child crying due to their best toy being broken, etc. This exercise will focus the children's minds on the non-verbal communication linked with human feelings, bearing in mind that a large proportion of our interaction with other human beings is through this medium, rather than through what we actually say.

All of the art forms discussed can also be extremely valuable in helping a grieving child to work through their feelings and express their loss. They are relevant as re-active techniques in the circumstances of bereavement, to help children express and deal with their feelings. Table 8 summarises the opportunities which schools can provide for helping children in the area of loss.

Table 8: Opportunities at school

Assemblies
Discussions
Sharing
Feelings
Listening

Caveat

It is important after exercises considering negative feelings, that things are concluded and closed in a positive manner. The children must never be left in a state of feeling negative, left to dwell on negative thoughts which may worry them.

Each exercise must be taken to its natural conclusion, ensuring all the children's questions have been answered and no ends are left untied. The teacher should then call the class together for a whole class discussion on something positive, such as something fun that is happening later that day or week.

The lesson focus should then be moved to an area enjoyed by the children, such as PE or music, which will help to restore a balance after the period relating to negative feelings.

The feelings of animals

Although facial expression and gesture are seen as typical of human communication, animals also have forms of communicating their feelings to each other. These can make an interesting discussion, such as the contrast in meaning when a cat or dog wags their tail, one showing pleasure and the other anger. Other forms of animal communication can be listed and discussed, including the snorting of horses, purring of cats, and the play fighting between young cubs.

There is always the danger of being too anthropomorphic, that is of assigning human emotions to animals. The teacher must be careful to avoid this and explain that we do not really know what an animal is feeling, but merely make assumptions based on our own responses in similar circumstances.

Follow-up Activities

1. How would you describe the links generally between home and school?
2. If there are any problems, how can these be addressed?
3. Do you address the issue of feelings in the classroom already? If so, how?
4. Is the issue of death addressed in your school? What are the most positive aspects of your home-school links?

CHAPTER 5
Science Topics

Ourselves

The topic area of 'ourselves' presents many opportunities for children to observe and understand the concept of change and cycles of development. The children themselves will have changed physically since they were first born, and they will have experienced other changes during their life, such as starting primary school, moving up through the classes, etc. Later they will move onto secondary school, then perhaps college and later still to starting work. Life is constantly moving and is a dynamic rather than a static experience.

Children may have great problems relating to ideas presented in theoretical and abstract manner. The more that children can relate these difficult concepts being taught to their own experiences in life, the better the chance that they will internalise these concepts and really begin to understand them. The younger the child the greater is the impact of their own life experiences, in learning new concepts.

The topic of 'ourselves' should begin on a simple level, perhaps with the children looking back to their own infancy. They can ask their parents to tell them what they were like as babies and collect photographs of themselves from when they were babies through to the present. If they bring the photos into school, include a game of guessing which baby photograph belongs to which child. Other teachers and staff in school could also join in by lending photographs. The children could also discuss with their classmates things which they can remember from when they were very young and compare these with their observations of younger siblings and friends.

These experiences can be extended into other mediums, such as writing, drawing or painting about their earlier life experiences. The project can be continued by the children looking forward to the next stages in their life. Through this they will hopefully start to gain a conceptual insight into both the cycles and stages of life.

The topic can always be extended into a broader investigation of the children's families, with parents, grandparents and siblings being considered. They can discuss what each generation in their family currently do, whether at school, college, work or retired. It should be possible for the children to construct a family tree, including photographs, drawings or a combination of both.

Children enjoy discussing favourite foods and drinks and these can be investigated with an emphasis on why we need to eat and why we need a balanced diet. Discussions can include comparing the children's diets with those of children in other countries, or those of animals. From a physiological point of view the skeletons of animals and humans can be examined and drawn, including skulls, teeth and other bones. The reasons for the skeleton framework could be considered, as well as the changes in the form of growth as we gain weight and height after birth. The children will indirectly gain an appreciation of death and the cycle of change as the skeletons are modelled on the bone structure of once living creatures.

Encourage the children to think in terms of the future and to articulate their thoughts as to what they expect they will be doing in the future. Younger children will initially talk about what they will be doing at the weekend as their concept of time is not yet fully developed. Gradually move on to discussing predictions for the weeks, then the months ahead. The children may well be able to look forward and predict in relation to special events, such as Christmas, birthdays and holidays.

Make a life-map or time line of the years through from baby, infant, junior, teenager and adult. Look at the changes which occur during these stages in life and ask the children to make suggestions for their own life-plans. Begin by listing important past events that have already been experienced, then plot possible important events in the future, based on observations of older children, siblings and other relatives.

The professionals involved throughout the various life stages could be invited into the school to talk and work with the children on this topic. These may include health visitors, doctors, vicars and nurses. In addition, old age pensioners could be invited to the school to talk with the children about their life experiences. The children can discuss how these experiences differ from their own. It is important that thought, planning and good preparation are given careful attention when having guests at the school. Some visitors may not be used to talking to young children or may not be aware the general topic being studied. They should be well briefed before the visit and the children should prepare their questions beforehand. It is a good idea to use a tape recorder or video camera for the talk and following questions, to keep a permanent record of the visit which can be referred back to.

This sort of study, involving visitors, can also be linked with other areas of the curriculum, for example a history project. It may be possible for the school to create an active link between part of the community and the school. This could be a pensioners' home, which will provide the children with an opportunity to visit elderly citizens, and for them to visit the school for Christmas entertainment, harvest festivals, etc.

Changes

The seasons, change and the cycle of the year can all be good starting points with which to approach the areas of changes and losses in the curriculum. Through the study of change, the children will be helped to gain the concept of life being in stages and cycles, including the changes of birth, growth and death.

The idea of change itself can be explained on a very simple level. One example is by boiling a kettle of water, allowing the children to watch the water emerging as it changes into the vapour of steam. Another example is to watch ice cubes melt, changing from a solid to a liquid, or a slice of bread turning mouldy.

Over a longer period of time the children can observe change by sowing their own seeds and watching them grow, or by watching a vase of flowers gradually wilt and then die.

These and other observations can be linked with the project on 'ourselves', as the children can observe changes in their own life, including growth, over a period of time.

The seasons

Spring

Most children find it relatively easy to relate to the experiences of changing life cycles around them and usually have some general idea of the changing seasons. Some children, especially those with specific learning difficulties, may have problems with these temporal sequences and will need additional support in this area.

The seasons can be traced by the children, throughout the year, beginning with the starting point of new life in the spring. The children can record the weather, temperatures, wind direction and rainfall throughout the season, possibly throughout the whole year. These could then be stored on a computer or manually to record the seasons' changes and progression. They may include photographs, video recordings and tape recording with the more traditional recording methods.

During the progression of spring the days will gradually become longer, and the nights shorter. The climate slowly becomes warmer and often much damper. Children can gain valuable first-hand experience by being given the opportunity to plant their own seeds, taking an active part in caring for them. They will learn the conditions which seeds and plants need in order to grow and thrive.

Not all plants will thrive in all the conditions tested, and therefore a percentage will die. This will provide an ideal opportunity to observe and discuss death in nature.

Nature walks in the local environment, during spring time, will reveal the beginning of new growth. The children can observe the environment slowly being renewed after the previous desolation of winter. They can record their findings in writing or drawings, which may be compared with differences later in the year.

Environmental walks will obviously be far easier if the school is in a rural setting, though in an urban environment there will still be opportunities in local parks, school grounds, allotments and other public areas. The changes that have begun following winter can be readily observed; the growing buds on trees, green shoots emerging from the ground and so on. Birds will be beginning to build nests, eventually laying their eggs and producing a new generation. Some eggs may fall from their nests, or fledglings may be blown from the trees. Children are likely to notice these and again this provides a natural lead to talking with them about death. Discussions should be encouraged and any questions the children ask should be answered sensitively, honestly and in terms which the children can understand.

Observations made on the nature walks can be followed with discussions of changes the children have noticed in their own gardens, or in their pets at home. They may have noticed animals waking after going into hibernation. A visit to a farm during spring will give children further opportunities to see new life emerging, with the birth of lambs, chicks, etc. If the visit is repeated later in the year, when the animals have grown, the children will notice the changes in growth which will have taken place. An incubator could be brought into school to enable the children to observe hatching chicks. There may also be suitable contacts in the local community who can arrange to bring in young rabbits, lambs or chicks, preferably with the parent animal for comparison.

Summer

After spring you may wish to continue tracing the seasons, moving onto the summer months. The children can continue to record the weather and should notice that the climate becomes warmer and the days longer. The children may notice that they can play outside late into the evening during this time, in sharp contrast to the winter months.

With summer comes the period of farm harvesting and cropping. By harvesting their own crops, in the school grounds or classroom, the children will gain valuable first hand experience of looking after and cropping plants. Through such experiences the children will be able to observe the cycle of life from sowing the seeds, to cropping and eating the mature plants.

By continuing the nature walks the children can again observe seasonal changes; the blooming of flowers, ripening of crops, etc. One activity which can be very helpful is for the children to collect items on these walks to later classify back at school. They can be sorted into three categories, once living, still living and never living. Include dead twigs, stones, glass, paper and insects which can be carefully returned, unharmed. Ambiguous items, such as paper, can provoke interesting discussions.

Finally, the children may benefit from visiting local markets or supermarkets, to see the final stages in the crop cycle. Observe how the final produce is marketed and how different it appears from its start as a seed.

Autumn

The children's observations should be continued well on into the autumn season, a time when things in nature appear to decline. The children can observe the leaves falling from trees, vegetation turning from green to brown, final cropping and the gradual climatic changes in their environment. Temperatures will begin to fall while wind speed and rain measurements will increase.

Children will be aware of the debris as leaves and rubbish are blown about by the winds. They may even have been enlisted by their parents to help in clearing up the garden, perhaps making bonfires. What happens to all the garden rubbish they burn?

Examine old leaves and dead grass, etc. and compare these with their

earlier live state.
The days will be shortening and the children will notice that the
temperature is becoming cooler as winter slowly approaches.

Winter

The winter, being the final season, still presents opportunities for the
children to observe and record changes which are taking place in the
climate, as the temperatures become cooler and the days shorter. Nature
walks are still possible, this time to observe a much harsher and crueler
environment, with many trees devoid of leaves and the fields emptied
of their crops. Talk of hibernation and other ways in which animals
prepare themselves to survive the harsh winter conditions are also
relevant. Some animals, especially smaller ones and birds, will die during
this time, due to lack of food resources or the cold. Children are likely
to encounter these bodies, leading to further discussions about which
things are necessary for survival in nature's harsher environment. Again,
any questions raised about the death of these animals should be answered
honestly and with sensitivity.

Life cycles

Most animals have a much shorter life cycle than our own human life
cycle. Because of this, children can actually observe some parts of life
cycles in action over a relatively short period of time, within the
classroom environment. Sections of life cycles can be easily introduced
into the classroom to enable children to have much closer observation
of what is happening. It is through the study of life cycles, as well as
through other elements, that children can be helped to gain a gradual
insight into the natural cycles, changes and patterns of life and death
that exist all around them.

Frogs

The life cycle of the frog is an example frequently introduced into the
classroom of primary schools. Frog spawn can be kept in the classroom
and the changes observed by the children. They can observe the initial
spawn changing into tadpoles, then gradually through stages of growth
until the final metamorphose as the tadpoles change into frogs. The
children, as well as observing the development of the frog, can observe
the survival rate at each of the stages. This will give them the opportunity

to observe death first hand, which can then be discussed as a class. The adult frogs should always be carefully returned to their natural habitat.

Butterflies

The eggs of butterflies or moths can be kept in the classroom, though precautions must be taken to ensure that necessary food supplies are available. Changes can be observed as metamorphosis takes place from egg, to caterpillar, to pupa and finally to butterfly. These too should be released back into their natural habitat.
Butterflies can now be seen 'en masse' at butterfly farms and the various stages observed at very close hand. Since there are so many in number at each of the various stages, it is often possible to actually see changes from one stage to the next, which is a fascinating and memorable experience for the child.

Chickens

Part of the life cycle of a bird, the chicken, can be easily set up for observation in the classroom. This adds a good contrast to life cycles of amphibians and insects. An incubator needs to be borrowed, together with the necessary fertilised chicken eggs and the ancillary equipment such as heating, lights and food. It is likely that some of the eggs will not hatch, and that some of the chicks may not survive the early stage of life, which will allow for discussion about death with the children. The teacher needs to be prepared for any questions the children may ask and should not merely avoid the issue. As has been discussed, it is important for children to have these direct experiences and opportunities to begin building a concept of death. It is a valuable lesson for the children to learn and follow up discussions are essential to make sure they are not left with any negative or confused feelings.

Mammals

Mammals can offer opportunities to observe part of a life cycle in action, in the classroom. One common example is that of mice as they have a relatively short breeding cycle, as do rabbits. Guinea pigs have a lengthy gestation period, but the young are born precocious and are able to run about, in contrast with rabbits and mice whose young are heavily dependent after birth. The children may well have observed these

62

breeding cycles at home with their own pets, from cats and dogs to hamsters and guinea pigs. A farm visit will also present opportunities for the children to observe at least part of the life cycle of an animal. Visits can be arranged to see piglets, lambs and calves with their mothers.

Plants

Plants can be easily grown in the classroom or school grounds, so that children can observe their life cycles. Cress seeds can be planted by the children on water absorbent paper and with a little care and attention the crop will be ready within a few days. Sprouting beans can also be grown and observed in the classroom, as they have a relatively short cycle too. Sunflower seeds are fun to grow in various locations around the classroom and their growth can be measured over a period of time. They are particularly good as an example of a life cycle, because as they die their flowers produce visible seeds which they leave to begin a new cycle and a new generation. There could even be a class competition to see who can grow the tallest sunflower. Many other plants, such as the tomato, can be cultivated and observed indoors, or outside in the school grounds.

Life cycle stories

There are plenty of storybooks available to reinforce points based around life cycles. One example is 'The Very Hungry Caterpillar', though care should be taken to ensure the children do not take some of the eating habits of this caterpillar seriously!
There are more scientifically-based life cycle books available on both the frog and butterfly, as well as on many other creatures.

Length of life cycles

Different species of plants and animals can have varying lengths of life cycles. For example, trees tend to live far longer than annuals, just as horses tend to live longer than hamsters or mice.
All these differences can be investigated and used to help the children gain further insight into life and the cycle of change. Class pets or schools pets can also offer opportunities for the children to observe at least parts of the life cycles in action.
Visits to farms to see the young animals in their settings again reinforces the idea of life cycles, as does visiting places such as the butchers, as the

children may not have fully internalised the connection between the living animal and the dead meat!

Table 9 shows some of the themes possible for introducing life and death through the science curriculum.

Table 9: Science themes

Ourselves	Our past and our future
Relations	Lifelines
Helpers	Favourite things
Changes	Community links
The seasons	Pets
Life cycles	Animals
Insects	Plants

Follow-up Activities

1. Can you trace your life to date along a time line? Highlight both the low and the high points.
2. What do you think you will doing in five and ten years time?
3. A chick in a class incubator has died. A child asks what has happened. How would you respond? How would your reply differ if the child was a five, nine or twelve-year-old?
4. What is your favourite memory of your last holiday? Why?

CHAPTER 6
The Social Sciences

History

The study of recent history, especially that element relating to the sociological aspects of the subject, can be useful in helping children to gain an insight into the rhythms of life. A project relating to the second world war, for example, could include components such as the children recording the experiences of their grandparents, or even those of previous generations. Investigating things that these elder relations did, at a time when they were younger, will not only help to make the subject of history more understandable on a personal level, but will also be a reinforcement of the cycle of life in a context which the children can easily relate to. The children will be helped to gain an insight into the concept of time moving relentlessly forward and that their now elderly relations were once young like them. By implication, todays young children will eventually be elderly, replaced by new generations. Elements of history will link in with other subject areas, such as the study of past records. You could, for example, visit a local churchyard. The children may realise that in past times many people died during their childhood, and many others did not live beyond middle age. The effects of wars and plagues can be observed throughout the appropriate memorials. Much can be raised in discussion and related to the projects previously mentioned in the text.

Geography

Geography, and the study of land use, also offer the potential for discussion centred around such land uses as hospitals, nurseries, schools, old people's homes, churches and cemeteries. A study in this area can, at the appropriate level, move on into other areas including anthropology,

sociology, science and technology. The children could also study the
architecture of churches, the style and the materials that were used in
the construction of the building. This will also tie in with the previous
subject area of history. The church is often the oldest surviving building
in the area, and there are sociological questions which can be raised
relating not only to the use of the church, but also to the question of
why it has survived when so many other buildings have not. Many other
structures no longer remain intact, especially dwelling houses, with the
exceptions of structures of defence such as castles and city walls. Ancient
uses of the church such as of a sanctuary, along with the modern day
usage can also be investigated, linking in with the area of religious
education.

Recordings, taken through the medium of art, can also be made of the
church and churchyard, including rubbings of gravestones and
brassworks.

The flora and fauna in the churchyard can also be investigated and
recorded, linking in with other natural history projects.

The different shapes of the graves and the various symbols such as
crosses and angels adorning them, can be observed, recorded and
discussed. Discuss how the styles have changed over the various periods.
Other evidence can also be gathered, recorded and investigated, such as
collecting the epitaphs from gravestones. The children may like to make
up amusing epitaphs for fictional characters, pets or even themselves!

Imitation, stained glass windows could be built back in the classroom
as part of a technology project, as could investigations into the weights
that different shaped structures can bear, to test for the best shapes to
support heavy loads.

Archeology investigations may also reveal previous, abandoned sites
which former people occupied in past years, and this may also generate
further investigations into the reasons why these previous settlements
are no longer used. These inquiries may reveal reasons from the past,
such as that the village was deserted after the inhabitants died or fled
from the plague, or moved on when mineral workings were worked out.
These and other similar problems all demonstrate that although the
human species is relatively flexible and ingenious in many areas of life,
we are still vulnerable to nature and our environment. All of these things
provide an insight , as well as being starting points for further
investigations, discussion and debate.

Religious education

The study of religion, including those of the multi-cultural elements, provides the opportunity for children to investigate festivals, rituals and customs, not only from their own cultural background, but also those of other cultures both locally and abroad. Customs and celebrations of the rites of passage could be included in this study, including christenings, funerals, confirmations and their equivalents.

As with history, geography and land use, places of worship and other religions can be explored by the children.

Memorials to the dead can also be investigated, such as the war memorials dating from the first and second world wars, often found in village or town churchyards or parks. Some great buildings and structures can be discussed, such as the Taj Mahal, Pyramids, and the Wall of Remembrance in Washington DC, built in the memory of the soldiers killed in the Vietnam war. These investigations all tie in with topics in architecture and religious education.

The children can look at other memorials and ways in which the dead are remembered. This may include donated equipment to hospitals or charities, educational scholarships, plaques, etc.

There are other ways in which society as a whole remember the dead, as on Remembrance Day each November. The children could discuss the reasons for these public remembrances and the significance behind this remembering. Older children may also be interested in debating moral issues around death, such as that of euthanasia, or the conflict between Christianity and the Darwin-based theory of evolution. They may also be interested in discussing the purpose behind a funeral and how they view the choice between cremation and burial.

Music

Music fits conveniently into this area, linking with religious education, as it has been utilised in religious rites over thousands of years. Music includes rhymes and songs, as well as instrumental pieces, and can be a further way of demonstrating feelings.

The music used in religious ceremonies, celebrations, festivals and services can be investigated and the children can be given the opportunity to listen to various styles and to discuss their uses.

As discussed in the previous chapter, the children can explore different types of music in relation to feelings, using instruments to create their own music, depicting emotions.

Follow-up Activities

1. In which ways, if any, do you already address the area of loss and death through the arts?
2. How long do you think that Remembrance Day will continue in its present form? How relevant do you think it is now and how does it differ from 1945?
3. Are there any multicultural or ethnic implications to be considered in your school?
4. If so, has the area been addressed?
5. Think of your favourite piece of music. Why do you especially enjoy listening to it?

Part Three: The Re-active Approach

This part of the book addresses the situation where a bereavement has actually occurred within the community circle of the school. This could be when a child attending the school has had a person die, to whom they were closely attached, such as a parent or sibling. It may even be that a child at the school dies through an illness or accident.

The deceased may be a sibling, perhaps also on the school role, a parent or grandparent, or a member of the staff, though anyone with whom the child has had a close relationship can provoke a deep grief and mourning response.

The death may be sudden, or expected, and suggestions are provided as to how to react to each situation and where to seek additional help.

This section also looks at why it is important for the school to consider a whole school policy and joint response in the area of the reaction to death and bereavement. For example, parents and staff are likely to be in initial shock after news of the death and therefore a plan, at least in outline, is needed to ensure that matters are dealt with as effectively as possible rather than through crisis management.

CHAPTER 7
Short-term Reaction

Immediate support

The bereaved child potentially needs both immediate and also sympathetic support at school. School is a potential second family for many children, and it may also be a haven if the bereavement is causing problems and pressures at home. The parent-child relationship may be under extreme pressure, if a sibling or grandparent has died. In the case of a parent dying, there will potentially be a tremendous strain placed on the remaining parent, as they have to deal not only with their own grieving but also with that of their children. There is the danger that the bereft parent, and the children, may become quickly isolated following the initial period of support after the death and the funeral. The same could apply if there has been a tragedy involving children at the school. Whatever the situation, an appropriate, immediate response is vital and a system is needed to ensure follow up support.

Initial contact with parents

Ideally a designated person, such as the head teacher or class teacher, needs to make contact with the parents. Ideally this person should have some knowledge of counselling skills.

A sample of primary schools in Humberside rated the parents as the most important element in child bereavement, second only to the schools themselves. Clearly parents are crucial at this time and a good, solid relationship between the school and parents lays the foundation for a good initial response to the news of a death. This will hopefully continue until the child has made a full recovery from the bereavement.

If the parent initially contacts the school with news of the bereavement then thought needs to be given as to how the school should respond. At this point, only the briefest of details needs to be taken, as the home is likely to be in crisis and there will be many other arrangements which they need to make after the death. However, a link between the school and home should be established at this point, with the school offering a strong, supportive role. In addition, a promise should be made to contact the parents again at a later time when matters, such as the time and place of the funeral, have been resolved. It will be necessary to contact the parents again, within quite a short period of time, in order to finalise arrangements, such as attendance at the funeral.

The school needs to make a decision as to whether flowers will be sent to the funeral, or if a collection is to be made instead, taking into account the wishes of the bereaved.

There may also be cross religious or cross-cultural implications which would be useful for the school to understand. In this case, either the home or a religious contact will be able to provide details to assist the school.

Initially, though not necessarily, the child or children may be temporarily withdrawn from the school. The children may even be sent away to relatives or neighbours and advice may be sought from the school as to the suitability of including the children in any arrangements following the death. Advice on this has already been given, and will vary depending on culture, age and maturity. The general rule is that it is best, as far as possible, to include the children in any such arrangements, allowing the children some choice in matters such as viewing the body or attending the funeral. In general, children will be far more aware, and far more able to understand matters, than the adults around them anticipate and it is best to be truthful, within the understanding of the child.

The children will need to be given proper information to avoid the potential pitfalls, such as those of fantasy fears which are likely to be far greater than the reality. Information provided to the children should be at a level which the children can understand. Table 10 summarizes the immediate implications which the school needs to be aware of, after a bereavement, in relation to the family.

Table 10: Immediate support

Responding to the news
Contact with the parents
Acknowledgement
The funeral

Breaking the news

After obtaining brief details from the parents and arranging to make contact again later, the schools' next stage is communicating the news of the death to the rest of the staff and the children. First of all the news must be told to the staff and it is essential that all the adults are told, not just the teachers, in order to avoid potential embarrassment or giving the impression of being insensitive and tactless. The final step is telling the news to the children. It may seem easier to make a whole school announcement at an assembly, and certainly some sort of whole school acknowledgement will be both useful and positive. However, younger children and those children who are particularly close friends with the bereft child or the deceased child, should be told prior to this. These children should be told by their own teacher in the classroom setting, and the school needs to quickly identify these children who are going to need extra support. It is also important that these children are given time to respond to the bad news which they have just received, and for the teacher to be available to answer any immediate questions they may have. Any questions should be answered carefully, sensitively and tactfully, and teachers should not be afraid to admit if they cannot answer a particular point.

When these issues have been addressed, the whole school acknowledgement can take place, perhaps through an assembly. Bear in mind that anxiety levels may be raised in the other children, as hearing the news of a death brings the subject to their attention, in sharp focus. The children may, for a while, feel quite vulnerable and may also be concerned that they or members of their family may suddenly die. Table 11 summarizes some of the points regarding the breaking of news of a bereavement.

Table 11: Breaking the news

To all staff at the school
To the immediate friends of the child
To the younger children
To classmates
To the rest of the children in the school

This can also be a time of great stress for the staff at the school, who will be grieving themselves. With preparation, in terms of a strategic outline plan, and in terms of a positive school ethos, these effects will be minimised.

The media, such as the local press, may contact the school, and thought needs to be given as to how to respond to this type of approach. This aspect needs to be dealt with in a sensitive and tactful manner, preferably with the family's wishes taken into account. A decision needs to be made regarding who will be the spokesperson for the school in these circumstances. If the death or deaths have been traumatic, for example, if a group of children at the school have been killed in an accident, then the media are likely to attend 'en masse' to the discomfort and distress of staff and children. In these circumstances a far greater input, in terms of outside counselling for school members, will be necessary and matters will probably be on a far greater scale than for an individual bereavement.

The funeral

The next stage, at least in the short term, will include the funeral, which will probably take place within a week of the death. This may be quickly followed by the return of the child or children to school, although they may have returned before the funeral. The funeral is a watershed, a public rite of passage, a formal acknowledgement of the death which unfortunately may be regarded by many as a signal that the period of grieving is now at an end.

Ideally the school needs to have thought through the various options available with regard to the funeral, and also to have taken the various wishes of the parents into account. The options include who will represent the school at the funeral, whether to send flowers or make a collection and how the children of the school will be involved in these matters. With regard to flowers, it is obviously necessary to take the wishes of the family into account. This type of detail cannot be planned for, but it is still important to devise a plan which addresses each issue, a draft plan which forms the basis of a response by the school. Table 12 summarizes some of the key points regarding the funeral.

Table 12: The funeral

Who will attend, representing the school?
Flowers?
Collection?

The child returns to school

When the child first returns to school, the teacher can initially help to make things easier by sensitively acknowledging the fact of the loss and by providing time to listen to the child if they need to talk. It would be very insensitive, as well as counter productive, to adopt an interrogating approach. It may be difficult and painful for the child to talk about the bereavement. It may also be difficult for the teacher to reach out to the child, but this is a vital first step. The child must not feel isolated or unable to communicate, just as they should not feel uncomfortable about openly mourning their loss.

Similarly, the other children at school should not be discouraged or suppressed from talking about the death and talking to the child. This acknowledgement will be supportive and will help in the grieving process.

The scenario may arise that peers are reluctant to raise the subject of death with the bereaved child, which can lead them to feel rejected and alone, with their loss unacknowledged. Blackburn (1991) drew attention to the possibility that some children may feel quite alone with their grief, as the adults around them may assume that they are too young an age to really experience grief. It is important to provide the opportunity to listen to the child as much as possible. If it is not possible to hear the child immediately when a request is made, then the teacher should promise a time as soon as possible and make sure they keep to it. It is important to remember that the grieving process can take around two years from the time of the death to the resolution stage and that memories are always likely to remain. The emphasis at this early stage of grieving should be on both listening to and supporting the child as necessary and as appropriate.

Tempting though it may be to relate your own experiences to the child, and to offer platitudes such as, 'I know how you feel', these should be avoided. Nobody, except the bereaved themselves, can possibly know how they feel. To suggest this to a child merely devalues their loss.

The listener should have empathy with the child, but not pass judgement. In some cases it may become clear that further help is needed from a trained counsellor either on the school staff or through an agency.

Table 13: The child returns to school

Do acknowledge the loss.

Do reach out to the child.

Do listen.

Do take and make time.

Do avoid platitudes.

Do avoid relating own experiences.

Do not pressurise.

Remember that the child may feel alone and isolated.

Many schools in the Humberside studies previously mentioned, found that both the church and also the social services were useful during this initial stage of bereavement, as sources of advice and support. Other agencies which schools found helpful included the educational psychology service, educational welfare services, general practitioners, health visitors and voluntary counselling organisations, such as Cruse. The agency or person contacted first will depend on the previous experience of the school in dealing with such agencies, and any networks which the school already has in existence. Many agencies are potentially able to offer help to schools at these times of crisis and in case of a problem that the school cannot solve within its own resources. Similarly, if a second opinion is needed on any matters these agencies can be approached for advice.

Each of the areas where additional advice or support can be sought will specialise in different aspects of bereavement. For example, the church may be able to arrange a memorial service, the educational psychologist will be able to provide advice and help on behaviour problems that may arise in the future, and the counsellor will be able to suggest strategies to help the child to move through the process of grieving. Table 14 summarizes some of the sources of help available to schools.

Table 14: Sources of help

The church
Educational psychologists
Educational welfare officers
Social services
General practitioner
Health visitors
The voluntary sector eg. Cruse

Follow-up Activities

1. Do you have plans in place at school to deal with a bereavement crisis?
2. How would you break the news of the death of a child to their classmates?
3. Which agencies would you contact to help provide support after a bereavement?
4. Where do you intend to go on holiday next year?

CHAPTER 8

Medium-term Response

Memorials

In the medium term, the time of the funeral will have passed and the bereaved child will have returned to school. The school may like to commemorate the life of the deceased, particularly if it was a member of the school community. Some form of memorial may be appropriate, to remember the deceased, and may involve planting a tree or buying a bench for the school grounds. A memorial prize could be awarded annually for an activity which was enjoyed by the deceased. Funds could be raised by a collection from the school and from the local community. If a classmate has died then the other children in the class may like to write their own pieces of remembrance, to put together in a special remembrance book. The bereft child, whose parent or sibling has died, may also find this a useful and therapeutic exercise. Such books can include writings, poems, drawings, photographs and artefacts which belonged to the deceased. These activities are also VERY positive in terms of the grieving process.

Expression of feelings

Raphael (1984) suggested that some children may well have delayed their grief and actively need the help of the close adults around them. The adults need to help these children to express both their thoughts and feelings. By doing this they can help to guide the children towards the final resolution of their grief.
Grief may be delayed for a variety of reasons. In cases such as post traumatic stress disorder, specialist help should be sought. This will include cases where a child has witnessed a violent death or been one of a few survivors in a traumatic accident.

If there are no complicating factors such as these, then it may simply be that the bereft child finds it very difficult to articulate their feelings, in which case other mediums should be considered. These should help the children to order their thoughts, identify their feelings and by expressing them, work through their grief.

The use of writing, drawing, painting, drama and music are all mediums through which children can express their feelings, if they are having difficulty in verbalising them. Through such activities the teacher can slowly draw the children in to discussing their feelings, but again, the child must not be interrogated or pressured. They may find that making a scrap book or memory book, including photos of the deceased, is an alternative way of acknowledging their loss. It is important not only that the loss is acknowledged, but also that the grief is expressed. Good times and happy memories of the deceased should also be remembered and celebrated by the child. Table 15 summarises some of the ways in which children may express their feelings.

Table 15: Some ways of expressing feelings

Talking
Writing
Drawing
Painting
Drama
Music

Behaviour changes

The teacher may notice some behaviour changes in the bereft child at school, often reflecting the different stages of mourning mentioned earlier in the text. The teacher, along with the rest of the school staff, must be prepared to adopt a sympathetic but firm approach, while carefully liaising with the parents. Advice from other agencies should be sought, such as educational psychologists, if matters are not resolved or seem to be getting out of hand. Both the studies by Leckley in Belfast and Holland and Ludlow in Humberside showed that the majority of teachers noticed some behaviour changes in the bereaved children at school.

In nearly eighty per cent of the primary schools sampled in the Humberside study, teachers reported noticing either physical or psychological effects of bereavement, or a combination of both. Over forty per cent noticed that some of the children were displaying disruptive behaviour, anger or violence, all of these reflecting the anger and bewilderment stages of the early mourning period. About one third of schools in the study also reported that some of the children became withdrawn, showing signs of depression, again reflecting a stage in the process of mourning. Other signs of grieving which the schools identified included sadness, tearfulness, regression and apathy, to varying degrees. Another issue to be aware of is that the child may become very anxious not to be separated from their parents or siblings, fearing another death will occur while they are separated. Alternatively, if a parent has died, the child may seek a substitute or replacement quasi parent with whom to develop a close bond.

There are a multitude of reasons why children may overtly display these signs of mourning as they are working through their grief. The children may feel helpless or resentful that their parent or sibling has died, and in consequence may well react with depression, lethargy or anger. The children may now suddenly lack attention at home, especially if a sibling has died, or if a now sole parent is going through their own grieving process. Attention from other people, adult relations and friends, may now be focused on the parent or parents, so the child will not receive the time or energy they need. Here the child has, in a sense, suffered a double bereavement, not only the loss of a sibling or parent but also a loss of attention, and possibly comfort, from the surviving parent or parents.

Although some deterioration in school work was noticed in the studies mentioned, it was only in a small proportion of the bereaved children. The teacher should still be aware that the child may find it difficult to concentrate, being somewhat preoccupied with their own thoughts, especially in the very early stages of bereavement. It is also important throughout this period that the teacher is constantly prepared and able to provide a listening ear if that is what the child needs.

Special days

Some anniversaries and days of celebration can present problems for children which teachers should be aware of. They need to keep a special watch on the bereaved child during these times, as the child may temporarily regress in their grieving. The anniversary of the death of a parent, or sibling, may bring back painful memories for the child either directly themselves, or indirectly through their parents. Memories of the events that occurred at the time of the death may again be raised.

In addition, at times such as Christmas, the child may find the celebrations and merriment very difficult to deal with in terms of their own grief. It may all seem very unfair to the child. This will depend on the age of the child, and the period since death, as well as how far the child has progressed through their grief to the stage of resolution. Some regression may be anticipated at these times.

Birthdays too may be very sad occasions, with old memories of the deceased being revived and thoughts of 'what might have been'. This is mourning for a lost future. The child may experience this directly themselves, or indirectly through the grief of their family. Table 16 shows some of the times which may present difficult times for the child.

Table 16: Times to watch carefully

Anniversary of the death
Birthdays
Christmas

Follow-up Activities

1. Have you noticed any behaviour changes in a child which may relate to bereavement?
2. Do you have any procedures in place to remind you of potentially difficult anniversaries? If not, might such a system be of use?
3. Do you have any strategies in place to help the bereaved child at school?
4. Which of your birthdays do you remember with most pleasure, and why?

CHAPTER 9
Long-term Planning

The strategic plan

The logic in having a plan in place before an event has even occurred, is that some pre-crisis thought has been given to the subject, while people are in a clear and logical frame of mind. Such a plan does not have to be rigidly followed when the crisis does occur, but can offer simple guidelines and limit the likelihood of important issues being overlooked. A school plan for death and bereavement can be prepared at a time of calm, with all the staff having the chance to contribute. Some staff may possess special skills in the area, and therefore may be able to either lead discussions or contribute in a major way. If a plan is in place then there will be a framework to refer to, during a time of potential stress and trauma.

Having such an outline plan ready to put into operation will also avoid the chance of omissions during a crisis and things are less likely to be overlooked. Having a plan provides a secure framework from within which the school can act effectively.

Although it is obviously not possible to plan directly for every contingency, as each bereavement is itself unique, it is possible to plan some general strategies.

The plan should cover such points as who is to liaise with the parents in the initial and subsequent approaches, and how to break the news to the rest of the staff and to the children. Other things which need to be considered are how to acknowledge the loss of the child, dealing with both child and teacher grief, and which agencies can be approached for help if or when needed. Some thought could be given to the attendance at the funeral and whether to send flowers or have a collection, depending on the wishes of the family.

A sample of schools in the Humberside study, which had recent experience of dealing with a child bereavement, tended to have nominated staff who were responsible for this sensitive area of bereavement. In contrast, those schools who had not recently had any experience with a bereft child in the school had no key person responsible.

A key person with responsibility for bereavement at the school is an advantage. They are a resource for other staff to approach for advice and can monitor the strategic plan, though they may not necessarily be the person to approach the parents if a bereavement occurs. It may be that a more appropriate person is needed for this latter role, perhaps the class teacher who is more familiar with the family. Again, these are all issues for discussion by the staff as a whole.

In the unfortunate event of a death, and the plan having to be put into action, it is important that an evaluation is made of the response. Obviously not in the heat of the moment, although notes can be made for later consideration. A fuller evaluation needs to take place later, after things have calmed down, which will assist in the planning cycle and further help to improve future responses to bereavements.

Questions that need addressing

Although each bereavement is unique and does not easily fit into a general plan, it is advantageous to have some strategies in place. In the heat of the crisis of a sudden bereavement, the staff may themselves be in a state of shock. The fostering of good relationships between the school and parents is a strong foundation on which mutual trust can be developed, and as such is a crucial area which should be addressed.

With regard to the sudden death of a child at the school or a child at school being bereaved then the following questions could form the basis of a bereavement response document.

Policy questions

The following checklist suggests questions which can be raised to stimulate discussion before the preparation of a policy. The policy does need to be reviewed from time to time and must also be rigorously evaluated against its use to ensure that it is an effective plan.

82

Policy Checklist

1. Is one person on the staff to be solely responsible for the area of bereavement?
2. If there is not to be one person responsible for the area, will the responsibility be shared by all, or by a group of individuals?
3. Do persons selected have sufficient training?
4. If not, what training can be provided and on what time scale?
5. What training, if any, is needed generally for all staff in the area of child bereavement?
6. Who will be responsible for initially contacting the parents if there has been a death?
7. Who will be responsible for responding to the parents if they advise the school of a death?
8. Who will establish further links and liaise with the parents?
9. How will all the school staff, not just teachers, be told of the death?
10. How will the children be told the news, in classes, individually or jointly in assembly?
11. If the children are told in their classes, will a whole school acknowledgement also be made?
12. Who will identify children especially at risk, such as close friends of the dead child?
13. Who will monitor the bereaved children and those at risk?
14. Who will represent the school at the funeral?
15. Will flowers be sent to the funeral, or will a collection be made? Will this include staff and parents? Remember that the family of the bereaved may have their own wishes to take into account.
16. How will any cross-cultural or religious implications be identified and dealt with?
17. Which links have been established with other agencies to seek further help if necessary?
18. How will the child returning to school be monitored?
19. Can you think of any other short term considerations that may be overlooked in a crisis?
20. Who will write up a policy document and when will it next be reviewed?
21. How good generally are home-school relations? Can they be improved and if so how?

Bereavement Checklist

The list below applies equally to adults as to children and is a list of suggestions for interacting with a bereaved child. The basic rules are to interact with empathy and without making judgements.

1. Establish good home-school relationships, as good liaison will eliminate many problems.	
2. Avoid being afraid to reach out to a bereft child, and if necessary do make the first move.	
3. Avoid relating your own experiences to the child, or offering platitudes such as, 'I know how you feel'. It is fine just to say to the child that you are sorry about what has happened.	
4. Don't change the subject if you are approached by a bereft child wishing to talk about their experiences.	
5. Make a definite time to talk with the child during the day, if you cannot talk immediately.	
6. Do listen and, if necessary, seek the help of a trained counsellor.	
7. Don't be afraid of just listening, or of silences in conversations.	
8. Don't minimise the loss that the child has suffered by trying to find only positive elements around the bereavement.	
9. Reassure the child that grief and tears are a natural response of which they should not be embarrassed or ashamed.	
10. Don't indicate that the child could have done something to have avoided the death.	

11. Don't be afraid of asking how you can help.	
12. Don't make over-compensatory allowances for the bereft child at school.	
13. Don't underestimate the length of the grieving process.	
14. Don't be afraid to ask for help from others if you are unsure how to cope with a particular issue.	
15. Avoid the use of euphemisms such as, 'passed away', 'falling asleep', 'lost', or 'taken by Jesus'.	
16. Do be honest to avoid misleading or confusing the child. If unsure, say that you don't know but will try to find out.	
17. Do be especially aware at anniversaries, such as the first of the death, birthdays and special occasions such as Christmas.	
18. Do keep a special watch on the child throughout the next two years.	
19. Do keep other staff at school informed of matters relevant to their helping the child.	

INSET Days

There can be advantages in bringing in somebody from outside the staff to deliver training in the area of bereavement as they will have specialist knowledge and far wider experience. There are also advantages in one or two of the staff seeking outside school training, then passing on information to the rest of the staff.

Much depends on the objectives behind any training, whether it is to transmit general information and foster a greater awareness in the area, perhaps in preparation for a whole school approach to bereavement, or whether it is for selected staff to move further into the area of counselling skills.

In the former case, a member of staff with some knowledge in the area and using this book, including some of the exercises provided, could run an 'in house' course. The objectives of the course must be fully identified as the first step and later an evaluation should be made against these objectives.

The follow-up activities used at the end of the chapters are listed separately in the Summary of Follow-up Activities. The last question in each list is a 'cooling down' question and as such can be omitted or left until the end of the session.

86

Summary of Follow-up Activities

1. Can you remember when you first started school, primary or secondary? What were your feelings?
2. Brainstorm as many of life's potential losses as you can within three minutes.
3. How did you feel when you first left home to go to college or move into your own home?
4. Recall some of the happy memories you have of your first home.
5. Recall losing a much favoured object. Can you remember both your initial and subsequent feelings, as you realised that it was not going to be found?
6. Do you have negative feelings about the subject of death? If so, can you think of the reasons for this?
7. Is it easier discussing death with a close relative, close friend or stranger? If there is a difference, can you think of a reason why?
8. Think of a special object or souvenir that you have. Why is it special to you?
9. Can you remember what you were told about death as a young child? What was your first source of information?
10. What can you recall about the first funeral you attended? How old were you? Was it what you had expected and what were your feelings?
11. If you have attended a funeral more recently, in which ways was the experience different and in which the same?
12. Which television programme have you most recently enjoyed and why?
13. How would you describe the links generally between home and school?
14. If there are any problems, how can these be addressed?
15. Do you address the issue of feelings in the classroom already? If so, how?
16. Is the issue of death addressed in your school?
17. What are the most positive aspects of your home-school links?

18. Can you trace your life to date along a time line? Highlight both the low and high points.
19. What do you think you will be doing in five and ten years time?
20. A chick in a class incubator has died. A child asks what happened. How would you respond? How would your reply differ if the child was a five, nine or twelve-year-old?
21. What is your favourite memory of your last holiday and why?
22. In which ways, if any, do you already address the area of loss and death through the arts?
23. How long do you think that Remembrance Day will continue in its present form? How relevant do you think it is now and how does it differ from 1945?
24. Are there any multi-cultural or ethnic implications to be considered in your school?
25. If so, has the area been addressed?
26. Think of your favourite piece of music. Why do you especially enjoy listening to it?
27. Do you have plans in place at school to deal with a bereavement crisis?
28. How would you break the news of the death of a child to their classmates?
29. Which agencies would you contact to help provide support after a bereavement?
30. Where do you intend to go on holiday next year?
31. Have you noticed any behaviour changes in a child, which may relate to bereavement?
32. Do you have any procedures in place to remind of potential difficult anniversaries? If not, might such a system be of use?
33. Do you have any strategies in place to help the bereaved child at school?
34. Which of your birthdays do you remember with most pleasure and why?

88

Bibliography

Useful addresses
Cruse, Cruse House, 126 Sheen Road, Richmond, Surrey TW9 1UR.
National bereavement support agency.
Gingerbread, 35 Wellington Street, London WC2. Single parent
support agency.
Society of Compassionate Friends, 6 Denmark Street, Bristol, BS1
5DQ. An international organisation for bereaved parents.
Social Services: see telephone book or local contact.

References
Adams, R. (1992) *'Bereaved and bewildered'* Times Educational
    Supplement 30-10-92.
Berry, N. (1992) *'Softening the blow: how one family coped with the
    death of their baby'*
Bereavement Care 11, 2 pp 18-19.
Bending, M. (1993) *'Caring for bereaved children'* Cruse; Richmond.
Blackburn, M. (1991) *'Bereaved children and their teachers'*
Bereavement Care 10, 2 pp 19-21
Black, D. (1993) *'Supporting bereaved children and families'* Cruse,
    Richmond.
Bornstein, P. E., Clayton P. J., Halikas, J. A., Maurice, W. L., Robins,
    E. (1973) *'The depression of widowhood at three months'* British
    Journal of Psychiatry, 122, 561-566.
Bowlby, J. (1973) *'Attachment and loss vol 2: separation'* Hogarth;
    London.
Department for Education (1994) *' Code of Practice on the
    Identification and Assessment of Special Educational Needs'*
Department for Education, London.
Department of Education and Science (1978) *'Special Educational
    Needs' (The Warnock Report)* H.M.S.O., London
Holland, J. M. (1993) *'Child bereavement in Humberside primary
    schools'* Educational Research 35, 3
Holland, J. M. and Ludford, C. (1995) *'The effects of bereavement on
    children in Humberside secondary schools'* British Journal of
    Special Education: 22,2

Kane, B. (1979) '*Children's concepts of death*' Journal of Genetic Psychology pp 134-141

Kubler-Ross, E. (1982) '*On death and dying*' Tavistock, London.

Lansdown, R. & Benjamin G. (1985) '*The development of the concept of death in children aged 5-9 years*' Child: Care, Health and Education, 11, pp 13-20

Leckley, J. (1991) '*Attitudes and responses to death education of a sample of primary school teachers in Belfast*' Bereavement Care 10, 2 pp 2-23

Lewis, C. S. (1961) '*A grief observed*' Faber and Faber.

Litten, J. (1991) '*The English way of death: the common funeral since 1450*' Robert Hale

Marris, P. (1974) '*Loss and change*' Routledge, London.

Parkes, C. M. (1987) '*Studies of grief in adult life*' International Press, Madison

Raphael, B. (1984) '*The anatomy of bereavement: a handbook for the caring professions*' Hutchinson, London.

Walter, T. (1990) '*Funerals and how to improve them*' Hodder & Stoughton

Ward, B & Associates (1989) '*Good Grief Good Grief*', Uxbridge

Worden, W. (1984) '*Grief counselling and grief therapy*' Tavistock

Watson, R. (1986) '*The only survivor*' Bereavement Care 5, 2 pp 19-20

Wells, R. (1988) '*Helping children cope with grief*' Sheldon, London.

Zach, H. (1978) '*Children and death*' Social Work Today 9 (39)

List of books for children relating to death and loss.

Briggs, R. (1980) '*The Snowman*' Weston Wood.

Carle, E. (1974) '*The very hungry caterpillar*' Hamilton.

Hughes, S. (1984) '*Dogger*' Bodley Head.

Lewis, C.S. (1961) '*A grief observed*' Faber and Faber.

Stickney, D. (1984) '*Waterbugs and dragonflies: explaining death to children*' Mowbray.

Varley, S. (1985) '*Badgers parting gift*' Anderson

Viorst, J. (1971) '*The tenth good thing about Barney*' Collins.